First World War
and Army of Occupation
War Diary
France, Belgium and Germany

32 DIVISION
Divisional Troops
Highland Light Infantry
16th (Service) Battalion (2nd Glasgow) Pioneers
1 March 1918 - 28 February 1919

WO95/2385/3

The Naval & Military Press Ltd
www.nmarchive.com
Published in association with The National Archives

Published by

The Naval & Military Press Ltd

Unit 10 Ridgewood Industrial Park,

Uckfield, East Sussex,

TN22 5QE England

Tel: +44 (0) 1825 749494

www.naval-military-press.com

www.nmarchive.com

This diary has been reprinted in facsimile from the original. Any imperfections are inevitably reproduced and the quality may fall short of modern type and cartographic standards.

© Crown Copyright
Images reproduced by permission of The National Archives, London, England, 2015.

Contents

Document type	Place/Title	Date From	Date To
Miscellaneous	WO95/2385 32 Division 16th Btn Highland Light Infantry March 1918-Feb 1919		
Heading	32nd Division Divl Troops 16th Bn Highland Lt Infy (Pioneers) 1918 Mar-1919 Feb From 97 Bde 32 Div To 9 Div Troops From 97 Bde 32 Div.		
Heading	32nd Divisional Troops. 16th Battalion Highland Light Infantry Pioneers March 1918. Dec 18		
Heading	16th Highland Light Infantry War Diary Volume XXIX 1st March To 31st March. Vol 28		
War Diary	Boesinghe	01/03/1918	31/03/1918
Heading	Pioneers. 32nd Div. War Diary 16th Battn. The Highland Light Infantry April 1918		
Heading	War Diary Of The 16th Battalion The Highland Light Infantry. Volume XXX. From 1st To 30th April 1918 Vol 29		
War Diary	Douchy-Les-Ayette	01/04/1918	02/04/1918
War Diary	Corps Reserve Line	03/04/1918	26/04/1918
War Diary	Fosseux.	27/04/1918	30/04/1918
Heading	To 'A' Headquarters 32nd Division.	01/06/1918	01/06/1918
Heading	War Diary Of The 16th Battalion The Highland Light Infantry (Pioneers). Volume XXXI. From 1st To 31st May. 1918 Vol 30		
War Diary	Fosseux	01/05/1918	06/05/1918
War Diary	Blaireville.	07/05/1918	20/05/1918
War Diary	X.3.C.9.4	21/05/1918	31/05/1918
Heading	War Diary Of The 16th Bn. The Highland Light Infantry (Pioneers) Volume XXXII. 10 To 30th June, 1918. Vol 31		
War Diary	X.3.C.9.4	01/06/1918	25/06/1918
War Diary	X.8.a.8.9	26/06/1918	30/06/1918
Heading	War Diary Of The 16th Highland Light Infantry Volume XXXIII. 1st To 31st July 1918. Vol 32		
War Diary	X.8.a.8.9	01/07/1918	01/07/1918
War Diary	X.8.a.5.9	02/07/1918	06/07/1918
War Diary	Warluzel	07/07/1918	19/07/1918
War Diary	Meichen Camp	20/07/1918	25/07/1918
War Diary	Roykens Akker	26/07/1918	31/07/1918
Heading	War Diary Of The 16th Battalion The Highland Light Infantry Volume XXXIV. 1st to 31st August 1918. Vol 33		
War Diary	Roykens Akker	01/08/1918	05/08/1918
War Diary	Scout Camp Near Proven	06/08/1918	07/08/1918
War Diary	Longpre	08/08/1918	08/08/1918
War Diary	Domart-Sur La-Luce	09/08/1918	09/08/1918
War Diary	Beaucourt	10/08/1918	10/08/1918
War Diary	Le Quesnel	11/08/1918	12/08/1918
War Diary	Cayeux	13/08/1918	13/08/1918
War Diary	Berteaucourt Sur-La-Luce	14/08/1918	18/08/1918
War Diary	Warfusee-Abancourt	19/08/1918	20/08/1918
War Diary	Harbonnieres	21/08/1918	28/08/1918

War Diary	Framerville	29/08/1918	29/08/1918
War Diary	Ablaincourt	30/08/1918	31/08/1918
Heading	War Diary of The 16th Battalion The Highland Light Infantry Volume XXXV. 1st To 30th September 1918		
War Diary	Ablain-Court	01/09/1918	05/09/1918
War Diary	Misery	06/09/1918	07/09/1918
War Diary	Devise	08/09/1918	08/09/1918
War Diary	Tertry	09/09/1918	12/09/1918
War Diary	Villers Brettoneux	13/09/1918	17/09/1918
War Diary	Athies	18/09/1918	24/09/1918
War Diary	Tertry	25/09/1918	28/09/1918
War Diary	Vermand	29/09/1918	30/09/1918
Heading	War Diary of the 16th Battalion The Highland Light Infantry. Volume XXXVI. 1st-31st October. 1918		
War Diary	Bellenglise	01/10/1918	07/10/1918
War Diary	Beaumetz	08/10/1918	23/10/1918
War Diary	Bohain	24/10/1918	31/10/1918
Heading	16th Battalion The Highland Light Infantry War Diary November, 1918. Volume XXXVII. Vol 36		
War Diary		01/11/1918	30/11/1918
Heading	War Diary of the 16th Battalion The Highland Light Infantry. Volume XXXVIII. From 1st To 31st December, 1918		
War Diary	Cerfontaine	01/12/1918	05/12/1918
War Diary	Florennes	06/12/1918	06/12/1918
War Diary	Bioul	07/12/1918	07/12/1918
War Diary	Naninnes	08/12/1918	14/12/1918
War Diary	Maillen	15/12/1918	31/12/1918
Heading	Lancashire Division (Late 32nd Divn). 16th Bn. High'd Lt Infy (Pioneers) Jan-Feb 1919		
Heading	War Diary of the 16th Battalion The Highland Light Infantry. Volume XXXIX. From 1st to 31st. January 1919		
War Diary	Maillen.	01/01/1919	31/01/1919
Heading	War Diary of the 16th Battalion The Highland Light Infantry. Volume XL. From 1st To 28th February 1919		
War Diary	Nameche.	01/02/1919	01/02/1919
War Diary	Rheindorf	02/02/1919	11/02/1919
War Diary	Dottendorf	12/02/1919	25/02/1919
War Diary	Solingen	26/02/1919	28/02/1919

WO95/2385

32 Division

16th Btn Highland Light Infantry

March 1918 – Feb 1919

32ND DIVISION
DIVL TROOPS

16TH BN HIGHLAND LT INFY (PIONEERS)

~~MAR - DEC 1918~~

1918 MAR — 1919 FEB

From 97 BDE 32 DIV

To 9 DIV TROOPS

From 97 BDE 32 DIV

32nd Divisional Troops.

16th BATTALION

HIGHLAND LIGHT INFANTRY

Pioneers

MARCH 1918

- 16th HIGHLAND LIGHT INFANTRY -

- WAR DIARY -

- VOLUME XXIX -

- 1st MARCH TO 31st MARCH -

WAR DIARY
or
INTELLIGENCE SUMMARY.

Vol. XXIX

Army Form C. 2118.

Place	Date	Hour	Summary of Events and Information	Remarks and references to Appendices
BOESINGHE	1st March 1918		In Huts nr to BOESINGHE	wef/t
do	2nd		do.	wef/t
do	3rd		do.	wef/t
do	4th		do.	wef/t
do	5th		do.	wef/t
do	6th		do.	wef/t
do	7th		do.	wef/t
do	8th		do.	wef/t
do	9th		do.	wef/t
do	10th		do.	wef/t
do	11th		do. Intermittent shelling of camp.	wef/t
			Casualties Killed 1 O.R. and 4 Horses. Wounded 1 O.R.	

Army Form C. 2118.

WAR DIARY
or
INTELLIGENCE SUMMARY.
(Erase heading not required.)

Place	Date	Hour	Summary of Events and Information	Remarks and references to Appendices
BOESINGHE	12th March		"En Hutments", BOESINGHE. Intermittent shelling of camp, no casualties	w.e/f-
do	13th "		do do	w.e/f-
			Casualties	
			Wounded 2 Other Ranks	
do	14th		"En Hutments", BOESINGHE. Intermittent shelling of camp, no casualties	w.e/f-
do	15th		do do do	w.e/f-
do	16th		do do	w.e/f-
do	17th		do do	w.e/f-
do	18th		do 2nd Lieut. H.O. McKENZIE joined the Battalion from 6th Bn High L.I.	w.e/f-
do	19th		do	w.e/f-
do	20th		do Casualties	w.e/f-
			Wounded 2 other ranks (gas).	
do	21st		"En Hutments" BOESINGHE. Battalion Headquarters moved to PIONEER CAMP.	w.e/f-
			which had been built by the Battalion in its leisure time during the Month.	
			"En Hutments", "PIONEER CAMP", BOESINGHE. BOESINGHE CAMP Shelled.	
do	22nd		Casualties Wounded 1. O.R.	w.e/f-

A 5834 Wt. W4973/M687 750,000 8/16 D. D. & L. Ltd. Form/C.2118/13.

WAR DIARY
or
INTELLIGENCE SUMMARY.
(Erase heading not required.)

Army Form C. 2118.

Place	Date	Hour	Summary of Events and Information	Remarks and references to Appendices
BOESINGHE	23rd March		In "PIONEER CAMP", BOESINGHE	w/f
do	24th "		do do do	w/f
do	25th "		do do do	w/f
do	26th		do do do	w/f
do	27th		do do do	w/f
do	28th		In "PIONEER CAMP" BOESINGHE. Moved from BOESINGHE CAMP to PESELHOEK STATION where the Battalion entrained for TINCQUES. Marched from TINCQUES to Billets in BEAUFORT.	w/f
do	29th		In Billets at BEAUFORT do. do. en route for front line.	w/f
do	30th		In Billets at BEAUFORT. The Battalion marched to Billets in GAUDIEMPRE the Battalion now being attached to 96th Inf. Bde as a fighting unit.	w/f
do	31st		in Billets at BEAUFORT. The Battalion moved to Brigade Reserve (96th Infantry Brigade) at line at DOUCHY-LES-AYETTE.	w/A

R. C. Boyle
Lieut-Colonel,
Commanding
16th Bn Highld. L.I.

Pioneers.
32nd Div.

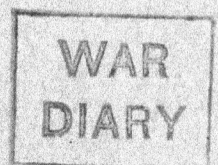

16th BATTN. THE HIGHLAND LIGHT INFANTRY.

A P R I L

1 9 1 8

32

Vol 29

28 P.
9 sheets

Confidential

War Diary

of the

16th Battalion The Highland Light Infantry

Volume XXX

From 1st to 30th April 1918

Army Form C. 2118.

Volume XXX   Page 1.

WAR DIARY
or
INTELLIGENCE SUMMARY.
(Erase heading not required.)

Instructions regarding War Diaries and Intelligence Summaries are contained in F. S. Regs., Part II. and the Staff Manual respectively. Title pages will be prepared in manuscript.

Place	Date 1918 April	Hour	Summary of Events and Information	Remarks and references to Appendices
DOUCHY-LES-AYETTE	1st		In Reserve to 96th Infantry Brigade at Sunken Road near DOUCHY-LES-AYETTE. Casualties: Killed 1 O.R. Wounded 2 O.R.	w.e.f.t
Do	2nd		In Reserve to 96th Infantry Brigade. The Battalion resumed duties as Divisional Reserve, and was quartered in trenches in vicinity of MONCHY-AU-BOIS and ADINFER WOOD. The Battalion was employed in building shelters in these trenches and constructing and improving trenches in Divisional Reserve Line, and in making Strong points in ADINFER WOOD.	w.e.f.t
CORPS RESERVE LINE	3rd		In Divisional Reserve in vicinity of MONCHY-AU-BOIS. The Corps Commander under authority of the Field Marshal Commanding-in-Chief has awarded the following Decoration for Gallantry and Devotion to duty in the Field. The Military Medal. No. 41007 Pte (A/Cpl) J. Calvin attached 97th T.M. Battery. Casualties: Killed 1 O.R. (accidentally)	w.e.f.t
CORPS RESERVE LINE	4th		In Divisional Reserve. Casualties: Wounded 7 O.R.	w.e.f.t

Army Form C. 2118.

WAR DIARY
or
INTELLIGENCE SUMMARY.

(Erase heading not required.)

Volume XXX Page 2

Instructions regarding War Diaries and Intelligence Summaries are contained in F. S. Regs., Part II. and the Staff Manual respectively. Title pages will be prepared in manuscript.

Place	Date	Hour	Summary of Events and Information	Remarks and references to Appendices
CORPS RESERVE LINE	5th		In Divisional Reserve in vicinity of MONCHY-AU-BOIS	welft
Do.	6th		In Divisional Reserve	welft
Do	7th		In Divisional Reserve. Casualties: Wounded 1 O.R.	welft
Do	8th		In Divisional Reserve. Casualties: Killed 2 O.R. Wounded 3 O.R.	welft
Do	9th		In Divisional Reserve. Casualties: Killed 6 O.R. Wounded 1 O.R.	welft
Do	10th		In Divisional Reserve	welft

Army Form C. 2118.

WAR DIARY
or
INTELLIGENCE SUMMARY.
(Erase heading not required.)

Volume XXX Page 3

Instructions regarding War Diaries and Intelligence Summaries are contained in F. S. Regs., Part II. and the Staff Manual respectively. Title pages will be prepared in manuscript.

Place	Date 1918 April	Hour	Summary of Events and Information	Remarks and references to Appendices
CORPS RESERVE LINE	11th		In Divisional Reserve in vicinity of MONCHY-AU-BOIS Casualties: Wounded 5 O.R.	w.e/t
Do	12th		In Divisional Reserve in vicinity of MONCHY-AU-BOIS Casualties: Wounded 10. O.R.	w.e/t
Do	13th		In Divisional Reserve Casualties: Wounded 3 O.R.	w.e/t
Do	14th		In Divisional Reserve Casualties: Wounded 3 O.R.	w.e/t
Do	15th		In Divisional Reserve Casualty: Wounded 1 O.R.	w.e/t
Do	16th		In Divisional Reserve. The Corps Commander under authority granted by the Field Marshal, Commanding in Chief has awarded the following Decorations for Gallantry and Devotion to Duty in the Field. The Military Medal. No 9997 Sergt F. Bothwell No 114543 Pte J. Taylor	w.e/t

Volume XXX Page 4

Army Form C. 2118.

WAR DIARY
or
INTELLIGENCE SUMMARY.

(Erase heading not required.)

Place	Date 1918 April	Hour	Summary of Events and Information	Remarks and references to Appendices
CORPS RESERVE LINE	17th		In Divisional Reserve in vicinity of MONCHY-AU-BOIS Casualties: Wounded 3 O.R.	w.e/f
Do.	18th		In Divisional Reserve	w.e/f
Do.	19th		In Divisional Reserve Casualties: Wounded 3 O.R.	w.e/f
Do.	20th		In Divisional Reserve Casualties: Wounded 1 O.R.	w.e/f
Do.	21st		In Divisional Reserve Casualties: Wounded 1 O.R.	w.e/f
Do.	22nd		In Divisional Reserve Casualties: Wounded 1 O.R.	w.e/f
Do.	23rd		In Divisional Reserve Casualties: Wounded 2 O.R.	w.e/f

WAR DIARY or INTELLIGENCE SUMMARY.

Army Form C. 2118.

Volume XXX Page 5

Place	Date 1918 April	Hour	Summary of Events and Information	Remarks and references to Appendices
CORPS RESERVE LINE	24th		In Divisional Reserve in vicinity of MONCHY-AU-BOIS. The Corps Commander wish Authority granted by the Field Marshal Commanding in Chief has awarded the following Decoration for Gallantry and devotion to duty in the Field. <u>The Military Medal</u> N.O.14396 Pte. G.J.Ross. Casualties: Wounded 1 O.R.	appx
Do	25th		In Divisional Reserve	appx
Do	26th		In Divisional Reserve. The Battalion moved in motor lorries to Camp at FOSSEUX, transferred to Third Army Reserve. Headquarters Officers were accommodated in Billets A1, A2, A3, and A6 in the village, the remainder of the Battalion being in Adrian and Nissen huts at P.16.central Sheet 51.C.	appx
FOSSEUX	27th		In huts, tents and Billets in FOSSEUX. The Battalion paraded at 12 noon for inspection by the Commanding Officer. Major General G.D.SHUTE, C.B., C.M.G. this day gave up command of the 32nd Division on promotion to command V Corps.	appx

Army Form C. 2118.

WAR DIARY
or
INTELLIGENCE SUMMARY.
(Erase heading not required.)

Volume XXX   Page 6

Instructions regarding War Diaries and Intelligence Summaries are contained in F. S. Regs., Part II. and the Staff Manual respectively. Title pages will be prepared in manuscript.

Place	Date	Hour	Summary of Events and Information	Remarks and references to Appendices
FOSSEUX	1918 April 27th		He called to take leave of the Commanding Officer, and complimented him on the appearance and achievements of the Battalion. "You have always been one of the best Battalions in the Division" he said "But as Pioneers you are absolutely at the top of the tree." The following order was afterwards received from him:— To all ranks 32nd Division. Good-bye and good-luck to the 32nd Division. I cannot tell you how I hate leaving you with whom I have been so long and who have fought so splendidly. You have always played up and have never been downhearted and I want you all to know how great my admiration for you is. My promotion is due entirely to your work and your gallantry. Again I congratulate you and thank you. (Sd) C.D. Shute. Major-General 27th April, 1918	w/f/f

Army Form C. 2118.

Volume XX Page 7

WAR DIARY
or
INTELLIGENCE SUMMARY.

(Erase heading not required.)

Instructions regarding War Diaries and Intelligence Summaries are contained in F. S. Regs., Part II. and the Staff Manual respectively. Title pages will be prepared in manuscript.

Place	Date 1918 April	Hour	Summary of Events and Information	Remarks and references to Appendices
FOSSEUX	28th		In Billets and Hutments in FOSSEUX. Church Parade was held at 12 noon this day — Officiating clergyman — The Rev. J. MacAdam, C.F. The O.R.E. inspected the Battalion and complimented them on the excellent work they had done during the last 28 days in the Reserve line.	w.e.f.
FOSSEUX	29th		In Billets and Hutments in FOSSEUX. Training Programme commenced. Parade 9am to 12.30pm. Recreational Training in the afternoon.	w.e.f.
FOSSEUX	30th		In Billets and Hutments in FOSSEUX. Training Programme continues.	w.e.f.

R. Coyle. Lieut Colonel
Commanding 16th Highland Light Infantry

30th April, 1918.

To 'A'.
  Headquarters.,
   32nd Division.

Herewith war
Diary for the month
of May.

  Dudw. McFarlane
   Capt. & Adjt. for
  Lt. Col. Comdg.

Vol 30

29 P
12 sheets

Confidential

War Diary
of the
16th Battalion The Highland Light Infantry (Pioneers)

Volume XXXI

From 1st to 31st May, 1918.

WAR DIARY or INTELLIGENCE SUMMARY

Army Form C. 2118.

Volume XXXI Page 1.

Place	Date	Hour	Summary of Events and Information	Remarks and references to Appendices
FOSSEUX	1918 May 1st		In Billets in FOSSEUX. Training continued. The new Divisional Commander, Major General. J. CAMPBELL, C.B, C.M.G, D.S.O, visited the Battalion this day, and expressed himself as greatly pleased with the type and general appearance of the men. Orders were received that in the event of immediate operations the Battalion should be prepared to move to LA CAUCHIE on receipt of orders from Division. A present was received from the Corporation of the City of GLASGOW consisting of equipment to complete a full Pipe Band for the Battalion: Pipes, Drums, Dirks, Sporrans, and Uniforms. A concert was given by "C" Company at 7pm.	
FOSSEUX	2nd		In Billets in FOSSEUX. The Battalion had a Route March this day at 9am. Route. FOSSEUX - BAVINCOURT - GOUY - FOSSEUX. When passing GOUY the Battalion was inspected by the VIth Corps Commander, Lieut General Sir AYLMER HALDANE.	

Army Form C. 2118.

Volume XXXI   Page 2

WAR DIARY
or
INTELLIGENCE SUMMARY
(Erase heading not required.)

Place	Date 1918 Mar	Hour	Summary of Events and Information	Remarks and references to Appendices
FOSSEUX	2nd		The following communication was received later from G.S.O.1, Division:— "I am desired to inform you that the Corps Commander was greatly pleased with the good turn out and smart bearing of the 16th Highland Light Infantry (Pioneers) today.	
FOSSEUX	3rd		In Billets in FOSSEUX. Training continued.	
FOSSEUX	4th		In Billets in FOSSEUX. Training continued	
FOSSEUX	5th		In Billets in FOSSEUX. Training continued. Church Parade at 9.30am, in concert Hut, the morning being wet. Officiating clergyman Rev. A. McHARDY, G.F. Major G.R.S. Paterson, M.C, and Lieut J.6atto posted to 2nd Bgh. L.I. on this date.	

Army Form C. 2118.

Volume XXXI Page 3

WAR DIARY
or
INTELLIGENCE SUMMARY

(Erase heading not required.)

Place	Date 1918 May	Hour	Summary of Events and Information	Remarks and references to Appendices
FOSSEUX	6th		In Billets in FOSSEUX. The Battalion moved from FOSSEUX to BLAIREVILLE. 'A' Company to RANSART. Working under VI Corps. The Chief Engineer addressed Officers of the Battalion, and accompanied by the C.O. and 2 Officers per company started taping out a new switch between HENDECOURT and AYETTE.	
BLAIREVILLE	7th		In Billets in BLAIREVILLE. 'A' Company in RANSART. Battalion started work on new switch and made satisfactory progress.	
BLAIREVILLE	8th		In Billets in BLAIREVILLE. 'A' Company in RANSART. Work on new switch continued	

Army Form C. 2118.

WAR DIARY
or
INTELLIGENCE SUMMARY

(Erase heading not required.)

Volume XXXI Page 4

Instructions regarding War Diaries and Intelligence Summaries are contained in F. S. Regs., Part II. and the Staff Manual respectively. Title Pages will be prepared in manuscript.

Place	Date 1918 May	Hour	Summary of Events and Information	Remarks and references to Appendices
BLAIREVILLE	9th		In Billets in BLAIREVILLE. "C" Company in RANSART. 2nd Lieut R. Young, A.C.M., M.M. joined Bn. from R.E. School ROUEN. Work on new switch continued.	
BLAIREVILLE	10th		In Billets in BLAIREVILLE. "A" Company in RANSART. Chief Engineer VI Corps and C.O. 10th D.C.L.I. 2nd Division (Pioneers) visited C.O. re their taking over our work on the 12th inst., our Division coming out to the line then to relieve the 2nd Division. The Battalion was visited by Major General BRIDGEWOOD who assumed command of the Division vice Major General CAMPBELL. Reinforcements joined Bn. 1 or.	
BLAIREVILLE	11th		In Billets in BLAIREVILLE. "A" Company in RANSART. The work on new switch being carried out under direction of Brig. General HARVEY, Chief Engineer VI Corps was handed over to 10th Bn D.C.L.I. (Pioneers). The Battalion this day started work in the Division area under the direction of C.R.E., 32nd Division.	

Army Form C. 2118.

WAR DIARY
or
INTELLIGENCE SUMMARY

(Erase heading not required.)

Volume XXXI Page 5

Instructions regarding War Diaries and Intelligence Summaries are contained in F. S. Regs., Part II. and the Staff Manual respectively. Title Pages will be prepared in manuscript.

Place	Date	Hour	Summary of Events and Information	Remarks and references to Appendices
BLAIREVILLE	1918 May 12th		In Billets in BLAIREVILLE. "C" Company in RANSART. Casualties: 1 O.R. wounded.	
BLAIREVILLE	13th		In Billets in BLAIREVILLE. "C" Company in RANSART. Lieut Colonel R. KYLE. D.S.O. proceeded to a conference at Third Army HQ on this date. Major W.D. Scott, D.S.O., M.C., assumed command of the Battalion. Casualties: 1 O.R. wounded.	
BLAIREVILLE	14th		In Billets in BLAIREVILLE. "C" Company in RANSART. Casualties: 1 O.R. wounded.	
BLAIREVILLE	15th		In Billets in BLAIREVILLE. "C" Company in RANSART.	

Army Form C. 2118.

Volume XXXI Page 6

WAR DIARY
or
INTELLIGENCE SUMMARY

(Erase heading not required.)

Instructions regarding War Diaries and Intelligence Summaries are contained in F. S. Regs., Part II. and the Staff Manual respectively. Title Pages will be prepared in manuscript.

Place	Date 1918 May	Hour	Summary of Events and Information	Remarks and references to Appendices
BLAIREVILLE	16th		In Billets in BLAIREVILLE "A" Company in RANSART. Captain R.D. BALLANTYNE and Lieut J. THOMSON returned from Hospital. Capt. R.D. BALLANTYNE joined the Divisional Depôt Battalion and took over command of "D" Company	
BLAIREVILLE	17th		In Billets in BLAIREVILLE "A" Company in RANSART Casualties: 1 O.R. wounded.	
BLAIREVILLE	18th		In Billets in BLAIREVILLE "A" Company in RANSART.	
BLAIREVILLE	19th		In Billets in BLAIREVILLE "A" Company in RANSART	

Army Form C. 2118.

WAR DIARY
or
INTELLIGENCE SUMMARY

(Erase heading not required.)

Volume XXXI Page 7.

Instructions regarding War Diaries and Intelligence Summaries are contained in F.S. Regs., Part II. and the Staff Manual respectively. Title Pages will be prepared in manuscript.

Place	Date 1918 May	Hour	Summary of Events and Information	Remarks and references to Appendices
BLAIREVILLE	20th		In Billets in BLAIREVILLE. "A" Company in RANSART. Owing to heavy hostile shelling Headquarters had to move from BLAIREVILLE to trenches West of village at point X.3.c.9.4., where Headquarters were constructed.	
X.3.c.9.4.	21st		In trenches at X.3.c.9.4. "A" Company in RANSART. An attack being considered imminent the Battalion occupied the Battle positions in the HAMEAU FARM locality at 2 a.m. As no attack developed the Battalion returned to trenches at X.3.c.9.4. at 5 a.m.	
X.3.c.9.4.	22nd		In trenches at X.3.c.9.4. "A" Company in RANSART. The Pipe Band performed at 3rd Bn. High. L.I. sports on the afternoon of 23rd May. Casualties: 2nd Lieut. R. BAIRD and 3 o.r. wounded.	

Army Form C. 2118.

WAR DIARY
or
INTELLIGENCE SUMMARY

(Erase heading not required.)

Volume XXXI Page 8.

Place	Date 1918 May	Hour	Summary of Events and Information	Remarks and references to Appendices
X.3.C.9.4.	23rd		In trenches in X.3.C.9.4. A Company in RANSART. Casualties: Wounded 1 O.R.	
X.3.C.9.4.	24th		In trenches in X.3.C.9.4. A Company in RANSART.	
X.3.C.9.4.	25th		In trenches in X.3.C.9.4. A Company in RANSART.	
X.3.C.9.4.	26th		In trenches in X.3.C.9.4. A Company in RANSART. Lieut. H.N.TAYLOR rejoined the Battalion from tour of duty in United Kingdom. Casualties: Killed 2 O.R. Wounded 5 O.R.	

WAR DIARY or INTELLIGENCE SUMMARY

Volume XXXI Page 7

Place	Date 1918 May	Hour	Summary of Events and Information	Remarks and references to Appendices
X.3.C.9.4.	27th		In trenches at X.3.C.9.4. "A" Company in RANSART. Lieut Colonel R. KYLE, D.S.O., returned from Conference at Third Army School on this date.	
X.3.C.9.4.	28th		In trenches at X.3.C.9.4. "A" Company in RANSART. The following extracts of those specially mentioned in Sir Douglas Haig's despatches of 7th April, appeared in London Gazette of 21st May Capt r.Q.M. R. Simpson No 14227 L/Cpl E. McEwen No 14637 R.Q.M.Sgt J. Fackney 2nd Lieut A.O. Sinclair transferred to Royal Air Force in United Kingdom. J. Fackney left for United Kingdom to attend a Quartermaster's Course at ALDERSHOT.	
X.3.C.9.4.	29th		In trenches at X.3.C.9.4. "A" Company in RANSART.	
X.3.C.9.4.	30th		In trenches at X.3.C.9.4. "A" Company in RANSART. Captain J.L.Girven and Lieut M.L. McInnes joined the Battalion from 97th Lomer Coy. Lieut H.H. Baie joined the Battalion from Divisional employ and assumed command of "B" Company vice Captain J.A. Trott wounded in Action. Casualties: Lieut (A/Capt.) J. Trott wounded in action.	

WAR DIARY or INTELLIGENCE SUMMARY

Army Form C. 2118.

Volume XXXI Page 10.

Place	Date	Hour	Summary of Events and Information	Remarks and references to Appendices
X.3.c.9.4.	1918 May 31st		In trenches at X.3.C.9.4. "A" Company in RANSART. Captain J.W.Reid proceeded to Third Army School as instructor. Captain J.L.Craven assumed command of A. Company vice Captain J.W.Reid to Third Army School.	

R.Kyle, Lieut Colonel,
Commanding 16th Highland Light Infantry

31st May. 1918

Confidential

WR 31

30 P.
12 sheets

War Diary

of the

10th Bn. The Highland Light Infantry (Pioneers)

Volume XXXII

1st to 30th June, 1918.

Army Form C. 2118.

WAR DIARY
or
INTELLIGENCE SUMMARY.

(Erase heading not required.)

Volume XXXII Page 1

Instructions regarding War Diaries and Intelligence Summaries are contained in F. S. Regs., Part II. and the Staff Manual respectively. Title pages will be prepared in manuscript.

Place	Date 1918 June	Hour	Summary of Events and Information	Remarks and references to Appendices
X.3.C.9.4	1st		In trenches at X.3.C.9.4. West of BLAIREVILLE. "F" Company in RANSART	
X.3.C.9.4	2nd		In trenches at X.3.C.9.4. "A" Company in RANSART. The following letter was received from Lieut. J.P.B.Robinson, D.S.O., A.A.&Q.M.G., 32nd Division:— My Dear Kyle, I have been asked to thank you for the performance of your Pipe Band at the Canadian Sports the other day. Everybody was highly delighted with their playing, especially some American Officers who were present and who had never heard the Pipes before. Yours sincerely, (Sd) J.P.B.Robinson	

Volume XXXII Page 2

Army Form C. 2118.

WAR DIARY
or
INTELLIGENCE SUMMARY.
(Erase heading not required.)

Instructions regarding War Diaries and Intelligence Summaries are contained in F. S. Regs., Part II. and the Staff Manual respectively. Title pages will be prepared in manuscript.

Place	Date 1918 June	Hour	Summary of Events and Information	Remarks and references to Appendices
X.3.c.9.4.	3rd		In trenches at X.3.c.9.4. West of BLAIREVILLE "J" Company in RANSART Casualty 1 O.R. Wounded	
X.3.c.9.4.	4th		In trenches at X.3.c.9.4. "J" Company in RANSART. The following Decorations have been granted by His Majesty the King:- The Military Cross Temp. Captain W.F. Gault Fisher Temp. Captain J. Macfarlane Casualties. Wounded 6 O.R. Brigadier General F. Lumsden, V.C. C.B., D.S.O., killed in Action was buried at BERLES-AU-BOIS on this date. The Pipe Band was present at the funeral. At the request of the Division the Battalion constructed a Celtic Cross and placed it on the grave.	
X.3.c.9.4.	5th		In trenches at X.3.c.9.4. "A" Company in RANSART	

Volume XXXII Page 3.

Army Form C. 2118.

WAR DIARY
or
INTELLIGENCE SUMMARY.

(Erase heading not required.)

Instructions regarding War Diaries and Intelligence Summaries are contained in F. S. Regs., Part II. and the Staff Manual respectively. Title pages will be prepared in manuscript.

Place	Date	Hour	Summary of Events and Information	Remarks and references to Appendices
X.3.C.9.4	6th		In trenches at X.3.C.9.4. West of BLAIREVILLE. "A" Company in RANSART. The trenches occupied by B Company were heavily shelled by 4.2's between 8.30 and 11 a.m. Casualties 6 O.R. Wounded.	
X.3.C.9.4	7th		In trenches at X.3.C.9.4. "K" Company in RANSART. Pte. Sand proceeded to Third Army School, FORT MAHON. 2nd Lieut O.C.W. Peterson rejoined the Battalion from Third Army Musketry School, FORT MAHON. Lieut R.M. Wilson transferred to United Kingdom to complete Medical Studies.	
X.3.C.9.4	8th		In trenches at X.3.C.9.4. "A" Company in RANSART.	
X.3.C.9.4	9th		In trenches at X.3.C.9.4. "A" Company in RANSART. Casualty killed 1 O.R. 2nd Lieut W.H.Kidd from Third Army School 2nd Lieut J.P. Mitchell to VI Corps Gas School	

Army Form C. 2118.

Volume XXXII Page 4.

WAR DIARY
or
INTELLIGENCE SUMMARY.

(Erase heading not required.)

Instructions regarding War Diaries and Intelligence Summaries are contained in F. S. Regs., Part II. and the Staff Manual respectively. Title pages will be prepared in manuscript.

Place	Date	Hour	Summary of Events and Information	Remarks and references to Appendices
X.3.C.9.4.	10th		In trenches at X.3.C.9.4. West of BLAIREVILLE. A. Company in RANSART	
X.3.C.9.4	11th		In trenches at X.3.C.9.4. A. Company in RANSART. The Billets of the Battalion were inspected by the Divisional Commander, Major General G.J. Lambert, C.B., D.S.O. He made a very minute inspection of the Officers' and men's billets and expressed himself well pleased with their condition.	
X.3.C.9.4	12th		In trenches at X.3.C.9.4. A. Company in RANSART	
X.3.C.9.4	13th		In trenches at X.3.C.9.4. A. Company in RANSART	

WAR DIARY or INTELLIGENCE SUMMARY

Army Form C. 2118.

Volume XXXII. Page 5

Place	Date	Hour	Summary of Events and Information	Remarks and references to Appendices
X.3.C.9.4.	14th		In trenches at X.3.C.9.4. West of BLAIREVILLE. "A" Company in RANSART. Casualty Wounded 1 O.R.	
X.3.C.9.4.	15th		In trenches at X.3.C.9.4. "A" Company in RANSART. Casualties Wounded 2 O.R.	
X.3.C.9.4.	16th		In trenches at X.3.C.9.4. "A" Company in RANSART.	
X.3.C.9.4.	17th		In trenches at X.3.C.9.4. "A" Company in RANSART. The following decorations have been awarded by His Majesty the King:- The Meritorious Service Medal No. 14263 C.S.M. William Rugby No. 14119 Sergt. Malcolm Beaton 2nd Lieut. J.P.Mitchell from VI Corps Gas School	

Army Form C. 2118.

Volume XXXII Page 6

WAR DIARY
or
INTELLIGENCE SUMMARY

(Erase heading not required.)

Instructions regarding War Diaries and Intelligence Summaries are contained in F. S. Regs., Part II. and the Staff Manual respectively. Title Pages will be prepared in manuscript.

Place	Date	Hour	Summary of Events and Information	Remarks and references to Appendices
X.3.C.9.4.	18th		In trenches at X.3.C.9.4 West of BLAIREVILLE. "A" Company in RANSART	—
X.3.C.9.4	19th		In trenches at X.3.C.9.4 "A" Company in RANSART. Under orders from 32nd Division the Battalion carried out a practice occupation of its Battle positions in the HAMEAU Defences. The whole Battalion was in position by 10.30pm. The G.O.C., 97th Infantry Brigade went round the dispositions with the Commanding Officer, and expressed himself as being greatly pleased with the quiet and expeditious way in which the practice had been carried out, and also the efficient manner in which the Defences were manned. Each company was dismissed by the G.O.C., as he completed inspecting it; the last company and Headquarters leaving at 12.10am 20/6/18 for Billets. Casualties 3 O.R. wounded.	—
X.3.C.9.4	20th		In trenches at X.3.C.9.4. "A" Company in RANSART. Casualty 1 O.R. wounded	—

Volume XXXII Page 7.

WAR DIARY
or
INTELLIGENCE SUMMARY

Army Form C. 2118.

Place	Date	Hour	Summary of Events and Information	Remarks and references to Appendices
X.3.C.9.4	21/01		In trenches at X.3.C.9.4. West of BLAIREVILLE. "A" Company in RANSART. Casualty Wounded 1 O.R.	nil.
X.3.C.9.4	22nd		In trenches at X.3.C.9.4. "A" Company in RANSART. Casualties Wounded 2 O.R.	nil.
X.3.C.9.4	23rd		In trenches at X.3.C.9.4. "A" Company in RANSART	nil.
X.3.C.9.4	24th		In trenches at X.3.C.9.4. "A" Company in RANSART. The following letter was received from the Division:- The Divisional Commander inspected the work carried out last night on the NEW RED LINE by the 16th H.L.I.(Pioneers). He directs me to inform you that he was much pleased with the progress made in one night and trusts that the 16th H.L.I. (Pioneers) will maintain this good standard of work. (Sd) A.E. Macnamara, Lt.Col., G.S., 32nd Division. The undermentioned Officers proceeded to VI Corps School:- 2nd Lieuts. W.E. McInnes, E.M.R. Heddle, J. Mann. 6 Casualties Wounded 2 O.R.	nil.

Army Form C. 2118.

WAR DIARY
or
INTELLIGENCE SUMMARY

(Erase heading not required.)

Volume XXII Page 8

Instructions regarding War Diaries and Intelligence Summaries are contained in F. S. Regs., Part II. and the Staff Manual respectively. Title Pages will be prepared in manuscript.

Place	Date	Hour	Summary of Events and Information	Remarks and references to Appendices
X.3.c.9.4.	25th June 1918		In trenches at X.3.c.9.4. West of BLAIREVILLE. "A" Company in RANSART. Under orders from the Division the Battalion moved from trenches at X.3.c.9.4. to SUNKEN ROAD at X.8.a.8.9. The following Officer joined the Battalion on this date :- Captain J.G. Hepburn, M.G. Major M.D. Scott, D.S.O., M.C., proceeded on leave on this date. The Pipe Band returned from Third Army School.	
X.8.a.8.9	26th		In Sunken road at X.8.a.8.9. N.E. of RANSART. "A" Company in RANSART. The Corps Commander under authority of the Field Marshal Commanding in Chief has awarded the following Decorations :- The Military Medal No. 40174 Private Angus Kennedy No. 43231 Private John Mackie	

Volume XXXII Page 9.

Army Form C. 2118.

WAR DIARY
or
INTELLIGENCE SUMMARY

(Erase heading not required.)

Instructions regarding War Diaries and Intelligence Summaries are contained in F. S. Regs., Part II. and the Staff Manual respectively. Title Pages will be prepared in manuscript.

Place	Date	Hour	Summary of Events and Information	Remarks and references to Appendices
X.8.a.8.9.	27th		In Surken Road at X.8.a.8.9. N.E. of RANSART. F.Company in RANSART. The following letter was received from Division:- The Divisional Commander wishes you to express to the Officers and Other Ranks employed on the construction of the new Main Line of Resistance Trench his satisfaction at the manner in which the work has been carried out. The rapidity with which this trench has been conducted shows good organisation on the part of the Officers in charge and intelligent and hard work on the part of all ranks employed, which reflects credit on their units. (sd) A.E. McNamara, Lieut-Colonel, General Staff, 32nd Division.	

Army Form C. 2118.

Volume XXXII Page 10

WAR DIARY
or
INTELLIGENCE SUMMARY

(Erase heading not required.)

Instructions regarding War Diaries and Intelligence Summaries are contained in F. S. Regs., Part II. and the Staff Manual respectively. Title Pages will be prepared in manuscript.

Place	Date	Hour	Summary of Events and Information	Remarks and references to Appendices
X.8.a.8.9.	28th		In Sunken Road at X.8.a.8.9. N.E. of RANSART. A Company in RANSART.	
X.8.a.8.9.	29th		In Sunken Road at X.8.a.8.9. N.E. of RANSART. A Company in RANSART. The following letter was received from the Division:- The 60th Commander visited the new line of Resistance throughout its length to FACTORY Trench locality. He has directed that all ranks concerned should be informed of his satisfaction of what he saw, especially the good work done on the new line of Resistance. The Divisional Commander relies on all ranks maintaining the same high standard of work for the remainder of the time in the line, handing our defences in as good a condition as possible to the Guards Division. (Sd) A. McNamara, Lieut Col, General Staff, 32nd Division. The undermentioned Officers proceeded to the Third Army School on the date :- Lieut S.M. Roberts. 2nd Lieut N. England. 2nd Lieut R.M. Hardy. Captain J.G. Stephenson 15th A.L.I.	

2449 Wt. W14957/M90 750,000 1/16 J.B.C. & A. Forms/C.2118/12.

Army Form C. 2118.

Volume XXXII Page 11

WAR DIARY
or
INTELLIGENCE SUMMARY

(Erase heading not required.)

Place	Date	Hour	Summary of Events and Information	Remarks and references to Appendices
X.8.a.8.9	1918 June 30th		In Sunken road at X.8.a.8.9 N.E. of RANSART "A" Company in RANSART The undermentioned Officer joined the Battalion on this date :- Lieut. H. A. Agnew from 15th H.L.I.	nil.

R. Coyle. Colonel.
Commanding 18th Highland Light Infantry

30th June. 1918

Vol 32

Confidential

War Diary
of the
16th Highland Light Infantry

Volume XXXIII

1st to 31st July 1918.

Army Form C. 2118.

Volume XXIII Page 1

WAR DIARY
or
INTELLIGENCE SUMMARY.

(Erase heading not required.)

Instructions regarding War Diaries and Intelligence Summaries are contained in F. S. Regs., Part II. and the Staff Manual respectively. Title pages will be prepared in manuscript.

Place	Date 1918 July	Hour	Summary of Events and Information	Remarks and references to Appendices
X.8.a.5.9	1st		In Sunken Road at X.8.a.5.9. N.W. of RANSART Sheet 51.C. "A" Company in RANSART	O.i.C.
X.8.a.5.9	2nd		In Sunken Road at X.8.a.5.9. N.W. of RANSART "A" Company in RANSART	O.i.C.
X.8.a.5.9	3rd		In Sunken Road at X.8.a.5.9. N.W. of RANSART "A" Company in RANSART	O.i.C.
X.8.a.5.9	4th		In Sunken Road at X.8.a.5.9. N.W. of RANSART "A" Company in RANSART	O.i.C.
X.8.a.5.9	5th		In Sunken Road at X.8.a.5.9. N.W. of RANSART "A" Company in RANSART	O.i.C.

Army Form C. 2118.

Volume XXXIII page

WAR DIARY
or
INTELLIGENCE SUMMARY.

(Erase heading not required.)

Instructions regarding War Diaries and Intelligence Summaries are contained in F. S. Regs., Part II and the Staff Manual respectively. Title pages will be prepared in manuscript.

Place	Date	Hour	Summary of Events and Information	Remarks and references to Appendices
X.8.a.5.9	1918 July 6th		In Sunken Road at X.8.a.5.9 N.W. of RANSART. "A" Company in RANSART. The Battalion moved from X.8.a.5.9 N.W. of RANSART to Billets in WARLUZEL on relief by 4th Bn Coldstream Guards (Reserve)	Cla.S.
WARLUZEL	7th		In Billets in WARLUZEL	Cla.S.
WARLUZEL	8th		In Billets in WARLUZEL. Training was commenced today	Cla.S.
WARLUZEL	9th		In Billets in WARLUZEL. Training continued	Cla.S.

WAR DIARY
INTELLIGENCE SUMMARY

Army Form C. 2118.

Volume XXXIII Page 3

Place	Date	Hour	Summary of Events and Information	Remarks and references to Appendices
WARLUZEL	July 10th		In Billets in WARLUZEL. Training continued. The following letter was received from 32nd Division:— The Divisional Commander has been asked by the Corps Commander at the request of the G.O.C. Guards Division to express to all units his appreciation of the manner in which the lines were handed over to the Guards Division at the recent relief, both as regards the work which had been done on the new defences, and in respect to the great cleanliness of the lines. (Sd) A.C. McNamara. Lieut Colonel, General Staff 32nd Division	Oct.1
WARLUZEL	11th		In Billets in WARLUZEL. Training continued.	Oct.1

Army Form C. 2118.

WAR DIARY
or
INTELLIGENCE SUMMARY.

(Erase heading not required.)

Volume XXIII

Instructions regarding War Diaries and Intelligence Summaries are contained in F. S. Regs., Part II. and the Staff Manual respectively. Title pages will be prepared in manuscript.

Place	Date 1918 July	Hour	Summary of Events and Information	Remarks and references to Appendices

WARLUZEL	12th		In Billets in WARLUZEL
			Training continued
			On this day the Battalion received a test "Turnout" from Division.
			Message received from Division — 6.17 pm
			Message sent to companies by runner — 6.20 pm
			Companies were at Rendezvous as follows:—
			   1st Company 6.55 pm
			   2nd Company 7.4 pm
			   3rd Company 7.15 pm
			The Battalion was ready with 1st Line Transport to march off in Battle order at 7.15 pm.
			The Battalion was under orders to move in 4 hours notice
				Olav?.

WARLUZEL	13th		In Billets in WARLUZEL Training continued	Olav.O

A 5834. Wt. W4973 M687 750,000 8/16 D. D. & L. Ltd. Forms/C.2118/13.

Volume XXXIII   Page 5

WAR DIARY
INTELLIGENCE SUMMARY

Place	Date Hour	Summary of Events and Information	Remarks and references to Appendices
WARLUZEL	1918 July 14th	In Billets in WARLUZEL. Lieut-General Sir Aylmer Haldane, K.C.B., D.S.O. Commanding VI Corps presented Military Crosses & Military Medal Ribbons to Officers and other ranks of the 32nd Division. He addressed the troops, two men from each Battalion being present. In the course of his remarks he stated that he was very proud to have the 32nd Division under his command. It was a fine Division and had done well during the two months just completed in the line. He was specially pleased with the magnificent work done in the defences by the Pioneers and other Battalions and other units of the Division. The troops then marched past the Corps Commander in Column of Route. While the Commanding Officer was waiting on the main road the Corps Commander after leaving the Divisional Commander stopped his car and called on the C.O. He personally congratulated him on the extraordinary good work done by the Battalion and stated that the 17th H.L.I. was the finest unit on parade today.	Appx.

Army Form C. 2118.

WAR DIARY
or
INTELLIGENCE SUMMARY.

(Erase heading not required.)

Volume XXIII Page 6

Instructions regarding War Diaries and Intelligence Summaries are contained in F. S. Regs., Part II. and the Staff Manual respectively. Title pages will be prepared in manuscript.

Place	Date	Hour	Summary of Events and Information	Remarks and references to Appendices
WARLUZEL	1918 July 15th		In Billets in WARLUZEL. Training continued.	Cav.P.
WARLUZEL	16th		In Billets in WARLUZEL. Training continued.	Cav.P.
WARLUZEL	17th		In Billets in WARLUZEL. Training continued.	Cav.P.
WARLUZEL	18th		In Billets in WARLUZEL. Training continued.	Cav.P.

WAR DIARY or INTELLIGENCE SUMMARY.

Army Form C. 2118.

Volume XXIII Page 7

Place	Date	Hour	Summary of Events and Information	Remarks and references to Appendices
WARLUZEL	1918 July 19th		In Billets in WARLUZEL. The Division having been transferred II Corps Second Army, the Battalion moved from WARLUZEL by motor omnibuses to DOULLENS Railhead, thence by tactical train to MEICHEN CAMP F.13.a.3.5. Sheet 27. near PROVEN	O.i.c.d.
MEICHEN CAMP	20th		In Corps Reserve in MEICHEN CAMP	O.i.c.d.
MEICHEN CAMP	21st		In Corps Reserve in MEICHEN CAMP. The Battalion constructed part of a light Railway between JOSSELHOEK and WATOU	O.i.c.d.

Volume XXXIII Page 8

WAR DIARY
INTELLIGENCE SUMMARY.

Army Form C. 2118.

Place	Date 1918 July	Hour	Summary of Events and Information	Remarks and references to Appendices
MEICHEN CAMP	22nd		In MEICHEN CAMP T.13.a.3.5. construction. At work on Light Railway, between POSSELHOEK and WATOU	Cloud.
MEICHEN CAMP	23rd		In Corps Reserve MEICHEN CAMP. At Light Railway work construction	Cloud.
MEICHEN CAMP	24th		In Corps Reserve MEICHEN CAMP. At Light Railway work construction	Cloud.
MEICHEN CAMP	25th		In Corps Reserve MEICHEN CAMP. The Battalion moved from MEICHEN CAMP to ROYKENS AKKER R.3.d.8.9. sheet 27 to come under orders of XIX Corps for work.	Cloud.

Army Form C. 2118.

Volume XXXIII Page 9

WAR DIARY
or
INTELLIGENCE SUMMARY.

(Erase heading not required.)

Instructions regarding War Diaries and Intelligence Summaries are contained in F. S. Regs., Part II. and the Staff Manual respectively. Title pages will be prepared in manuscript.

Place	Date 1918 July	Hour	Summary of Events and Information	Remarks and references to Appendices
ROYKENS AKKER	26th		In Billets in ROYKENS AKKER R.3.a.8.9. At work constructing Plank roads for Ammunition supply between WESTOUTRE and RENINGHELST	Cont.
ROYKENS AKKER	27th		In Billets in ROYKENS AKKER R.3.a.8.9. At work constructing Plank roads for Ammunition supply Constructing Tramway between ZEVECOTEN and DE BEER CABARET	Cont.
ROYKENS AKKER	28th		In Billets in ROYKENS AKKER R.3.a.8.9. At work constructing Plank roads for Ammunition supply Constructing Tramway between ZEVECOTEN and DE BEER CABARET	Cont.
ROYKENS AKKER	29th		In Billets in ROYKENS AKKER R.3.a.8.9. At work on Plank road and Tramway construction	Cont.

Army Form C. 2118.

WAR DIARY
or
INTELLIGENCE SUMMARY.

(Erase heading not required.)

Volume XXXII Page 10

Instructions regarding War Diaries and Intelligence Summaries are contained in F. S. Regs., Part II. and the Staff Manual respectively. Title pages will be prepared in manuscript.

Place	Date Hour	Summary of Events and Information	Remarks and references to Appendices
ROYKENS AKKER	1918 July 30th	In Billets in ROYKENS AKKER R.3.d.8.9. At work on Plank road and Jockney construction	Obed?
ROYKENS AKKER	31st	In Billets in ROYKENS AKKER R.3.d. 8.9. At work on Plank road and Jockney construction	Obed?

R Whyte, Lieut-Colonel,
Commanding 16th High. L. I.

P/32
VR 33

32 P.
9 sheets

Confidential

Anderson

War Diary

of the

16th Battalion The Highland Light Infantry

Volume XXXIV

1st to 31st August 1918.

32 P
9 sheets

WAR DIARY or INTELLIGENCE SUMMARY.

Army Form C. 2118.

Volume XXXIV Page 1

Instructions regarding War Diaries and Intelligence Summaries are contained in F. S. Regs., Part II. and the Staff Manual respectively. Title pages will be prepared in manuscript.

(Erase heading not required.)

Place	Date 1918 August	Hour	Summary of Events and Information	Remarks and references to Appendices
ROYKENS AKKER	1st		In Billets in ROYKENS AKKER near BOESHOEPE. The Battalion came under orders of Chief Engineer XIX Corps and was employed on making roads and forways in MONT KEMMEL Sector	
Do	2nd		In Billets in ROYKENS AKKER Employed on roads and forways	
Do	3rd		In Billets in ROYKENS AKKER Employed on roads and forways	
Do	4th		In Billets in ROYKENS AKKER Employed on roads and forways	
Do	5th		In Billets in ROYKENS AKKER The Battalion moved from ROYKENS AKKER to Hutments (SCOUT CAMP) near PROVEN	

Army Form C. 2118.

Volume XXXIV Page 2

WAR DIARY
or
INTELLIGENCE SUMMARY.
(Erase heading not required.)

Place	Date	Hour	Summary of Events and Information	Remarks and references to Appendices
SCOUT CAMP NEAR PROVEN	1918 August 6th		In Hutments in SCOUT CAMP (NEAR PROVEN). H.M. The King inspected detachments of the Division at HOSPITAL CAMP near POPERINGHE on this date.	
Do	7th		In Hutments in SCOUT CAMP (NEAR PROVEN). The Battalion entrained at PROVEN STATION at 6.10pm	
LONGPRE	8th		The Battalion detrained at LONGPRE Station at 5 am and bivouacked in a field near the station. The Battalion moved at 3pm by Bus and March route and bivouacked near DOMART-SUR-LA-LUCE. The 32nd Division came under orders of G.O.C. CANADIAN CORPS	
DOMART-SUR-LA-LUCE	9th		In Bivouacs near DOMART-SUR-LA-LUCE. The Battalion moved at 3pm and bivouacked near BEAUCOURT. The 32nd Division relieved the 3rd Canadian Division in the line on night of 9/10th August	

WAR DIARY or INTELLIGENCE SUMMARY

Army Form C. 2118.

Volume XXXIV Page 3

Place	Date 1918 August	Hour	Summary of Events and Information	Remarks and references to Appendices
BEAUCOURT	10th		In Bivouacs near BEAUCOURT. The Battalion moved at 4.30pm and bivouacked near LE QUESNEL. The Division took part in the General Advance on this date, the H.L.I. in Divisional Reserve.	
LE QUESNEL	11th		In Bivouacs near LE QUESNEL. The Advance was continued by the Division. The 32nd Division was relieved on night of 11/12th August by the 2nd Canadian Division.	
LE QUESNEL	12th		In Bivouacs near LE QUESNEL. The Battalion moved at 7am and bivouacked near CAYEUX.	
CAYEUX	13th		In Bivouacs near CAYEUX. The Battalion was attached to 97th Infantry Brigade Group and marched at 2pm to bivouacs to BERTEAUCOURT-SUR-LA-LUCE.	

Army Form C. 2118.

Volume XXXIV   Page 4

WAR DIARY
or
INTELLIGENCE SUMMARY.

(Erase heading not required.)

Place	Date 1918	Hour	Summary of Events and Information	Remarks and references to Appendices
BERTEAUCOURT -SUR-LA-LUCE	14th		In bivouacs in BERTEAUCOURT-SUR-LA-LUCE	
Do	15th		In bivouacs in BERTEAUCOURT-SUR-LA-LUCE	
Do	16th		In bivouacs in BERTEAUCOURT-SUR-LA-LUCE. Lieut-Colonel R. KYLE, D.S.O. proceeded on leave. Major W.D. SCOTT, D.S.O., M.C. assumed command of the Battalion	
Do	17th		In bivouacs in BERTEAUCOURT-SUR-LA-LUCE. The Battalion moved with 9th Brigade Group by Bus and March route to WARFUSEE-ABANCOURT and relieved 2nd Australian Pioneer Battalion. The 32nd Division came under orders of A.C.C., Australian Corps.	
Do	18th		In bivouacs in WARFUSEE-ABANCOURT	

Army Form C. 2118.

WAR DIARY
or
INTELLIGENCE SUMMARY.

(Erase heading not required.)

VOLUME XXXIV Page 5

Instructions regarding War Diaries and Intelligence Summaries are contained in F. S. Regs., Part II. and the Staff Manual respectively. Title pages will be prepared in manuscript.

Place	Date 1918 August	Hour	Summary of Events and Information	Remarks and references to Appendices
WARFUSEE-ABANCOURT	19th		In bivouac in WARFUSEE-ABANCOURT. Lieut T. ROBERTSON from 4th H.L.I. joined Battalion	
WARFUSEE-ABANCOURT	20th		In bivouac in WARFUSEE-ABANCOURT. The Battalion moved to bivouac near HARBONNIERES	
HARBONNIERES	21st		In bivouac in HARBONNIERES. The Battalion worked under orders of C.R.E. on trenches and wire in forward area. Wounded 1 O.T.	
	22nd		In bivouac in HARBONNIERES. Wounded 5 O.T.	
	23rd		In bivouac in HARBONNIERES. Wounded 6 O.T.	

Army Form C. 2118.

WAR DIARY
or
INTELLIGENCE SUMMARY.

(Erase heading not required.)

VOLUME XXXIV Page 6

Instructions regarding War Diaries and Intelligence Summaries are contained in F. S. Regs., Part II. and the Staff Manual respectively. Title pages will be prepared in manuscript.

Place	Date	Hour	Summary of Events and Information	Remarks and references to Appendices
HARBONNIERES	1918 August 24th		In bivouac in HARBONNIERES. The 32nd Division attacked successfully with Australian Corps on this date. "A" Company 16th H.L.I. at disposal of G.O.C. 97th Infantry Brigade and "C" Company at disposal of G.O.C. 95th Brigade for consolidation and making strong points. Wounded 1 O.R.	
Do	25th		In bivouac in HARBONNIERES. The Battalion worked under orders of C.R.E. on trenches and were in forward area. Wounded 2 O.R.	
Do	26th		In bivouac in HARBONNIERES. At work on trenches and wire in forward area	
Do	27th		In bivouac in HARBONNIERES. The 32nd Division continued the advance towards the SOMME. The Battalion worked under C.R.E. on repairing roads and making tracks for Horse and Motor Traffic.	

A5834 Wt.W4973 M687 750,000 8/16 D. D. & L.Ltd. Forms/C.2118/13.

Army Form C. 2118.

WAR DIARY
or
INTELLIGENCE SUMMARY.

Volume XXIV Page 7

Instructions regarding War Diaries and Intelligence Summaries are contained in F. S. Regs., Part II. and the Staff Manual respectively. Title pages will be prepared in manuscript.

(Erase heading not required.)

Place	Date	Hour	Summary of Events and Information	Remarks and references to Appendices
HARBONNIERES	1918 August 28th		In bivouacs in HARBONNIERES. The Battalion moved at 4.30pm and bivouacked near FRAMERVILLE	
FRAMERVILLE	29th		In bivouacs in FRAMERVILLE. The Battalion moved at 8.30am to Old GERMAN CAMP and trenches at STARRY WOOD S.8.C Sheet 66 (near VERMANDOVILLERS) The Battalion moved at 1.30pm and bivouacked near ABLAINCOURT	
ABLAINCOURT	30th		In bivouacs near ABLAINCOURT. The Battalion worked under orders of C.R.E. on roads in the forward area	

WAR DIARY
INTELLIGENCE SUMMARY

Army Form C. 2118.

Volume XXXIV Page 8

Place	Date	Hour	Summary of Events and Information	Remarks and references to Appendices
ABLAINCOURT	31st		In hutments near ABLAINCOURT. The Battalion worked on roads in the forward area between ABLAINCOURT and the SOMME	

31st August 1918

W.D. Scott
Major
16th High L.I.
Commanding

Confidential

P/32 WL 34

33 p
8 sheets

War Diary
of the
16th Battalion The Highland Light Infantry

Volume XXXV

1st to 30th September 1918

Army Form C. 2118

WAR DIARY
or
INTELLIGENCE SUMMARY

(Erase heading not required.)

VOLUME XXXV Page 1.

Instructions regarding War Diaries and Intelligence Summaries are contained in F. S. Regs., Part II. and the Staff Manual respectively. Title Pages will be prepared in manuscript.

Place	Date 1918 Sept	Hour	Summary of Events and Information	Remarks and references to Appendices
ABLAIN-COURT	1st		In bivouacs at S.18.c., sheet 62.c., near ABLAINCOURT. The Battalion was employed repairing and improving the roads Eastward in the Divisional area.	Army
Do.	2nd		In bivouacs near ABLAINCOURT. Work on repairing and improving roads continued.	Army
Do.	3rd		In bivouacs near ABLAINCOURT. Work on roads continued.	Army
Do.	4th		In bivouacs near ABLAINCOURT. Work on roads continued.	Army
Do.	5th		In bivouacs near ABLAINCOURT. The Battalion moved to trench system near MISERY on the left bank of the River SOMME. The Division crossed the SOMME and attacked the enemy on the East side. The Battalion assisted in erecting bridges across the SOMME at ST CHRIST and BRIE.	Army

Army Form C. 2118.

WAR DIARY
or
INTELLIGENCE SUMMARY

(Erase heading not required.)

Instructions regarding War Diaries and Intelligence Summaries are contained in F. S. Regs., Part II. and the Staff Manual respectively. Title Pages will be prepared in manuscript.

Place	Date 1918 Sept.	Hour	Summary of Events and Information	Remarks and references to Appendices
MISERY	6th		In bivouacs at V.31.c., Sheet 62.c. near MISERY. The Battalion was employed repairing roads East of the River SOMME. The following is an extract of a letter received from Division :- The Divisional Commander congratulates the 14th and 97th Brigade Groups on the excellent work done yesterday. The surprise of the enemy opposite MISERPIGNY showed splendid initiative by 15th H.L.I. The turning movements to encircle and clear BRIE and ST CHRIST and the crossing of the party of K.O.Y.L.I. opposite GIZANCOURT were admirably carried out. The manner in which troops pushed on to the GREEN line and the work of the artillery were first class. The repair of the minor crossings and especially of the BRIE and ST CHRIST bridges reflects the greatest credit on R.E. Companies and 16th H.L.I. Information of positions reached and of the situation was quickly and accurately transmitted.	
Do.	7th		In bivouacs near MISERY. The Battalion moved from MISERY to bivouacs near DEVISE at work on roads East of DEVISE.	
DEVISE	8th		In bivouacs at V.8.d.25.65. Sheet 62.c. near DEVISE. The Battalion moved and bivouacked near TERTRY. at work on roads East of TERTRY The following letter was received from C.R.E., 32nd Division :- I have received, through the Chief Engineer, Fourth Army, the following message from the Engineer in Chief, British Armies in France :- " General HEATH wishes to congratulate you upon the speed with the bridge's at BRIE and PERONNE have been pushed on" In forwarding this message to me the Chief Engineer, Fourth Army asks me to convey it to all concerned to whom the credit is really due	

VOLUME XXV Page, 3.

WAR DIARY
or
INTELLIGENCE SUMMARY

Army Form C. 2118

Place	Date 1918 Sept.	Hour	Summary of Events and Information	Remarks and references to Appendices
TERTRY	9th		In bivouacs near TERTRY. W.8.b.65.35. Sheet 62.c. at work on roads East of TERTRY.	
Do.	10th		In bivouacs near TERTRY. at work on roads East of TERTRY.	
Do.	11th		In bivouacs near TERTRY. at work on roads East of TERTRY. The Division left the Australian Corps and came under orders of G.O.C. IXth Corps.	
Do.	12th		In bivouacs near TERTRY. The Battalion moved by Motor Omnibus to Billets in VILLERS BRETONNEUX. Headquarters in Billet No.92, RUE DE MAIRIE. The following letter from Division was received from G.O.C. Australian Corps :- My Dear General, as your Division is now passed out of my Command, I want to send you a few line to express to you and to your troops my very sincere thanks for their splendid co-operation with this Corps, during the period that I have had the honour of having them with us. No Commander could have received more loyal, more energetic and more efficient service. Your capture of HERLEVILLE and its environs, your energetic drive which hustled the enemy out of the bend of the SOMME, your forcing of the crossings at BRIE and ST CHRIST by clever outflanking tactics and your unremitting pursuit of the enemy to and through HOLNON WOOD were all feats of arms of which your Division can be justly proud. I should like you also to accept and convey to all ranks an expression of the pride and pleasure which it has been to the Australian troops to be so closely associated with such a Gallant Division of the Motherland. Wishing you, your Staff and the 32nd Division continued success Yours very Sincerely, (sd) JOHN MONASH, Lieut General Comdg. Australian Corps	

Army Form C. 2118.

WAR DIARY
or
INTELLIGENCE SUMMARY.

VOLUME XXXV Page 4.

(Erase heading not required.)

Place	Date 1918. Sept	Hour	Summary of Events and Information	Remarks and references to Appendices
VILLERS BRETTON- EUX	13th		In billets in VILLERS BRETTONEUX. The following letter was received from Division. The Divisional Commander desires to congratulate and to thank all ranks on the completion of the work which has been carried to such success during the past month. Since the 7th August the Division has been engaged in continuous movement and in operations which will be always remembered with pride by those who took part in them and which have had a large share towards bringing the war to a successful conclusion. It has fought successful battles, it has advanced more than 20 miles in the face of the enemy, and it has forced the passage of the SOMME.	
Do.	14th		In Billets in VILLERS BRETTONEUX.	
Do.	15th		In Billets in VILLERS BRETTONEUX.	
Do.	16th		In Billets in VILLERS BRETTONEUX.	
Do.	17th		In Billets in VILLERS BRETTONEUX. The Battalion moved by Motors to Hutments in V.3.a., Sheet 62.c. near ATHIES.	

Army Form C. 2118.

WAR DIARY
or
INTELLIGENCE SUMMARY.
(Erase heading not required.)

VOLUME XXXV Page 5.

Instructions regarding War Diaries and Intelligence Summaries are contained in F. S. Regs., Part II. and the Staff Manual respectively. Title pages will be prepared in manuscript.

Place	1918. Sept	Hour	Summary of Events and Information	Remarks and references to Appendices
ATHIES	18th		In Hutments in V.3.a. near ATHIES.	
Do.	19th		In Hutments near ATHIES.	
Do.	20th		In Hutments near ATHIES.	
Do.	21st		In Hutments near ATHIES.	
Do.	22nd		In Hutments near ATHIES.	
Do.	23rd		In Hutments near ATHIES. The Battalion moved from ATHIES to bivouacs in W.1.b.9.0. near TERTRY	
Do.	24th		In Hutments near TERTRY	

Army Form C. 2118.

WAR DIARY
or
INTELLIGENCE SUMMARY.
(Erase heading not required.)

VOLUME XXV Page 6.

Instructions regarding War Diaries and Intelligence Summaries are contained in F. S. Regs., Part II and the Staff Manual respectively. Title pages will be prepared in manuscript.

Place	1918 Sept	Hour	Summary of Events and Information	Remarks and references to Appendices
TERTRY	25th		In bivouacs in W.1.b.9.0. near TERTRY.	
Do.	26th		In bivouacs near TERTRY.	
Do.	27th		In bivouacs near TERTRY.	
Do.	28th		In bivouacs near TERTRY. The Battalion moved to bivouacs in R.16.a.3.1. Sheet THORIGNY near VERMAND.	
Nr. VERMAND	29th		In bivouacs near VERMAND. The 46th Division crossed the ST QUENTIN CANAL and captured the HINDENBURG Line, advancing to their objective (Green line) East of LEHAUCOURT and MAGNY-LA-FOSSE. The 32nd Division then passed through the 46th Division and advanced to their objective (Red line) East of LE TRONQUOY - LEVERGIES - West of CHATAIGNIES Wood. Map Sheet THORIGNY. The Battalion was employed on making good the approaches to the bridges over the Canal, assisting in erection of bridges over Canal and repairing the roads East of the Canal.	

Army Form C. 2118.

WAR DIARY
or
INTELLIGENCE SUMMARY.

(Erase heading not required.)

VOLUME XXV Page 7.

Instructions regarding War Diaries and Intelligence Summaries are contained in F. S. Regs., Part II and the Staff Manual respectively. Title pages will be prepared in manuscript.

Place	Date	Hour	Summary of Events and Information	Remarks and references to Appendices
VERMAND	1918 Sept 30th		In bivouacs in K.16.a.3.1. near VERMAND. The Battalion moved to trench system at G.35.c.9.2. near BELLENGLISE Work on bridges and roads continued.	

30th September, 1918.

R. Boyle
Lieut-Colonel,
Commanding, 16th Highland Light Infantry

Vol 35

34 P
7 sheets

Confidential

War Diary

of the

16ᵗʰ Battalion The Highland Light Infantry

Volume XXXVI

1st – 31st October. 1918

Army Form C. 2118.

WAR DIARY
or
INTELLIGENCE SUMMARY.
(Erase heading not required).

VOLUME XXXVI. Page 1.
Instructions regarding War Diaries and Intelligence Summaries are contained in F. S. Regs., Part II. and the Staff Manual respectively. Title pages will be prepared in manuscript.

Place	Date 1918 Oct	Hour	Summary of Events and Information	Remarks and references to Appendices
BELLEN-GLISE.	1st		In trench system at G.35.c.9.2. sheet THORIGNY near BELLENGLISE.	
Do.	2nd		In Trench system at G.35.c.9.2. sheet THORIGNY near BELLENGLISE. The following letters were received from C.E. Australian Corps through C.R.E., 32nd Division :- "I would like to take this opportunity of again thanking all the units under my command, for the really splendid work which they have done during the past month, and in particular the Officers N.C.O's and men who constructed the Bridges over the SOMME, and the ST QUENTIN CANAL. The credit is entirely due to those who actually did the work." "The Commander-in-Chief wishes to express high appreciation of the good work done by the Engineer units of the Fourth army in the construction of temporary and permanent crossings over the River SOMME during the recent operations. The work was carried out with remarkable rapidity, sometimes under Machine Gun fire, and bombardment by gas shells." (sd) C.H. FOOTE, Brig-General, Chief Engineer, Australian Corps.	
Do.	3rd		In trench system at G.35.c.9.2. sheet THORIGNY, near BELLENGLISE.	

Army Form C. 2118.

VOLUME XXVI Page 2.

WAR DIARY
or
INTELLIGENCE SUMMARY.

(Erase heading not required.)

Instructions regarding War Diaries and Intelligence Summaries are contained in F.S. Regs., Part II. and the Staff Manual respectively. Title pages will be prepared in manuscript.

Place	Date	Hour	Summary of Events and Information	Remarks and references to Appendices
BELLEN- GLISE.	4th		In Trench System at G.35.c.9.2. sheet THORIGNY, near BELLENGLISE. The Battalion employed on roads East of BELLENGLISE. The following letters were received from 32nd Division :- "Following from General RAWLINSON begins AAA Please convey to 32nd Division my best congratulations and warm thanks for their gallantry and dash in their operations about SEQUEHART and the BEAUREVOIR line which is the last organised of the HINDENBURG System AAA. I wish all ranks the best of luck and further successes. Following message was received from the Corps Commander AAA WELL DONE 32nd AAA.	
Do.	5th		In trench System in G.35.c.9.2. sheet THORIGNY near BELLENGLISE The Battalion moved by march route to billets in BEAUMETZ sheet 62.c.	
Do.	6th		In billets in BEAUMETZ. The Battalion occupied in Training in the forenoon and Recreational Training in the afternoon.	
Do.	7th		In billets in BEAUMETZ.	
BEAUMETZ	8th		In billets in BEAUMETZ.	

Army Form C. 2118.

WAR DIARY
or
INTELLIGENCE SUMMARY.

(Erase heading not required.)

VOLUME XXXVI Page 3

Instructions regarding War Diaries and Intelligence Summaries are contained in F. S. Regs., Part II. and the Staff Manual respectively. Title pages will be prepared in manuscript.

Place	Date	Hour	Summary of Events and Information	Remarks and references to Appendices
BEAU-METZ	9th		In billets in BEAUMETZ.	
Do	10th		In billets in BEAUMETZ.	
Do.	11th		In Billets in BEAUMETZ.	
Do.	12th		In billets in BEAUMETZ.	
Do.	13th		In billets in BEAUMETZ.	
Do.	14th		In billets in BEAUMETZ.	
Do.	15th		In billets in BEAUMETZ.	
Do.	16th		In billets in BEAUMETZ. The Corps Commander under authority delegated by the Field Marshal Commanding in Chief has awarded the following decorations :- The MILITARY MEDAL No. 13181 Sergt G. SMITH No. 353501 Sergt W. MUIR. No. 43234 Pte J. GEDDES.	

Army Form C. 2118.

VOLUME XXXVI. Page 4.

Instructions regarding War Diaries and Intelligence Summaries are contained in F. S. Regs., Part II. and the Staff Manual respectively. Title pages will be prepared in manuscript.

WAR DIARY
or
INTELLIGENCE SUMMARY.

(Erase heading not required.)

Place	Date	Hour	Summary of Events and Information	Remarks and references to Appendices
BEAU-METZ.	17th		In billets in BEAUMETZ.	
Do.	18th		In billets in BEAUMETZ. The Battalion moved from BEAUMETZ to Trench system at BELLENGLISE.	
Do.	19th		In Trench system at BELLENGLISE.	
Do.	20th		In Trench system at BELLENGLISE. The Battalion moved from BELLENGLISE to Billets in BOHAIN.	
Do.	21st		In billets in BOHAIN The Battalion at work on roads East of BOHAIN.	
Do.	22nd		In billets in BOHAIN Work on roads continued.	
Do.	23rd		In billets in BOHAIN Work on roads continued.	

Army Form C. 2118.

WAR DIARY
or
INTELLIGENCE SUMMARY.
(Erase heading not required.)

VOLUME XXVI. Page 5.

Place	Date 1918. Oct.	Hour	Summary of Events and Information	Remarks and references to Appendices
BOHAIN	24th		In billets in BOHAIN. Training carried on in the forenoon. Recreational Training in the afternoon. The following letter was received from 32nd Division:- "On two occasions during the past week the Army Commander has seen Brigade Groups of the 32nd Division on the march, and he has informed the Divisional Commander that he was much struck by the turnout both of men and transport, and by the excellent march discipline which he looks upon as a pattern to the army. The Divisional Commander has the greatest pleasure in notifying this praise to all units and is sure that all ranks will do their utmost to maintain the highest standard	
Do.	25th		In Billets in BOHAIN. Training continued.	
Do.	26th		In billets in BOHAIN	
Do.	27th		In billets in BOHAIN	
Do.	28th		In billets in BOHAIN.	

Army Form C. 2118.

WAR DIARY
or
INTELLIGENCE SUMMARY.

(Erase heading not required.)

VOLUME XXVI Page 6.

Instructions regarding War Diaries and Intelligence Summaries are contained in F. S. Regs., Part II. and the Staff Manual respectively. Title pages will be prepared in manuscript.

Place	Date	Hour	Summary of Events and Information	Remarks and references to Appendices
BOHAIN	29th		In billets in BOHAIN.	
Do.	30th		In billets in BOHAIN.	
Do.	31st		In billets in BOHAIN. The Battalion moved to billets in ST SOUPLET.	

Lieut-Colonel,
Commanding 16th Highland Light Infantry

31st October, 1918.

Vol 36

35P
10 sheets

16th Battalion The Highland Light Infantry.

War Diary.

November, 1918.

Volume XXVII.

Army Form C. 2118.

WAR DIARY
or
INTELLIGENCE SUMMARY.

(Erase heading not required.)

Volume XXVII page 1.

Place	Date	Hour	Summary of Events and Information	Remarks and references to Appendices
	November.			
	1st.		In billets in St. SOUPLET.	
	2nd.		Do. Do.	
	3rd.		Do. Do.	
	4th.		In billets in St. SOUPLET. The three Companies of the Battalion proceeded on the night of 3/4th November to construct in conjunction with the three Field Companies R.E. bridges across the SAMBRE - OISE Canal, for the passage of the Infantry Units of the Division who were to attack at dawn on the 4th November. During the bridging operations the enemy's artillery fire was extremely violent and the fire from M.G. machine guns on the opposite bank of the Canal about 30 yards away was very intense. 'A' and 'C' Companies especially took heavy casualties, but the behaviour of all ranks was such that the bridges were thrown across in record time enabling the Infantry to attack with success at zero hour. The casualties during the bridging operations were:-	
			Killed in Action	
			Lieutenant R. M. HARDY. 12 Other Ranks.	
			Wounded in Action.	
			Lieutenant F. MIDDLEMISS. 2nd Lieutenant J. MOWAT. 2nd Lieutenant J. L. YOUNG, D.C.M., M.M. 17 Other Ranks.	

Army Form C. 2118.

WAR DIARY
or
INTELLIGENCE SUMMARY.
(Erase heading not required.)

Place	Date	Hour	Summary of Events and Information	Remarks and references to Appendices
	November.			
	5th.		In billets in St. SOUPLET. The Battalion moved to billets in SAMBRETON. The following wire was received from Division:- Following from IX Corps begins AAA Following from General RAWLINSON AAA Please convey to 32nd Division my congratulations and warm thanks for their success to-day AAA The strong opposition they met with on the Canal and the determined way in which they overcame it and forced the passage is deserving of high praise AAA Ends AAA The Corps Commander desires to add his most cordial congratulations to the Army Commander's message AAA Please communicate to all ranks AAA Ends **Casualties** Wounded in action 2 other ranks.	
	6th.		In billets in SAMBRETON.	

WAR DIARY
or
INTELLIGENCE SUMMARY.

(Erase heading not required.)

Army Form C. 2118.

Place	Date	Hour	Summary of Events and Information	Remarks and references to Appendices
	November.			
	7th.		In billets in SAMBRETON. The Battalion moved to billets in FAVRIL. Under authority granted by His Majesty the King, the Field - Marshal Commanding -in - Chief has awarded the folowing decoration :- **THE MILITARY CROSS.** T/Lieutenant F. MIDDLEMISS.	
	8th.		In billets in FAVRIL. The Battalion moved to billets in GRAND FAYT.	
	9th.		In billets in GRAND FAYT.	
	10th.		In billets in GRAND FAYT. The Battalion moved to billets in AVESNELLES.	

WAR DIARY
or
INTELLIGENCE SUMMARY.
(Erase heading not required.)

Army Form C. 2118.

Place	Date	Hour	Summary of Events and Information	Remarks and references to Appendices
	November.			
	11th.		In billets in AVESNELLES.	
			Following message from 32nd Division begins AAA Hostilities will be stopped on the whole front at 1100 (French time) AAA Allied troops until further orders will not pass the line reached at this stage and this hour AAA Ends. Defensive measures will not be relaxed AAA There will be no intercourse with the enemy.	
			Extract from FOURTH ARMY circular No.G.S.125. dated 11th November,1918. The FOURTH ARMY has been ordered to form part of the Army of Occupation on the RHINE in accordance with the terms of the Armistice. The march to the RHINE will shortly commence, and, although carried out with the usual military precautions, will be undertaken generally as a peace march.	
	12th.		In billets in AVESNELLES.	
			The following letter was received from Division :- The conclusion of the Armistice with GERMANY brings to an end a period of victorious advance by the Division of which all ranks may justly be proud. Since 8th August the Army has advanced its line over more than 70 miles and of these the 32nd Division has been in the front line for more than 50 miles. Five times we have successfully broken the enemy's main defences, including the passages of the SOMME and of the SAMBRE and OISE Canal, and the destruction of the BEAUREVOIR-FONSOMME trenches of the HINDENBURG Line. During these operations the Division has captured more than 2,700 prisoners, 60 guns, 500 machine guns and great quantities of war material. During most of its advance the Division has been opposed by some of the best troops which the enemy could put in the field. None of its victories have been gained without hard fighting in which the individual efforts of Officers and men have been put to the highest test.	

WAR DIARY
or
INTELLIGENCE SUMMARY.

(Erase heading not required.)

Army Form C. 2118.

Place	Date	Hour	Summary of Events and Information	Remarks and references to Appendices
	November. 12th.		The letter from 32nd Division (continued).	
			The Divisional Commander desires to thank all ranks of his Staff and of all Units for the response they have at all times made to his direction. He believes that never in the world's history has the reputation of a unit in a great army deserved to stand higher and he knows that whatever orders may be given for the future they will be carried out with the same determination devotion, and spirit that has given to the Division its present distinguished position.	
			(sd) E. Dillon, Lieut-Colonel, General Staff, 32nd Division.	
			12th November, 1918.	
	13th.		In billets at AVESNELLES. The Battalion moved to billets at Q.3.a.2.5 (sheet 57) on the AVESNELLES - SAINS- Du- NORD Road.	
	14th.		In billets at Q.3.a.2.5 on the AVESNELLES - SAINS Du NORD Road.	
	15th.		In billets at Q.3.a.2.5. The Battalion moved to billets in LIESSES. Headquarters in Chateau de la Motte.	
	16th.		In billets in LIESSES.	

Page 6.

Army Form C. 2118

WAR DIARY
or
INTELLIGENCE SUMMARY
(Erase heading not required.)

Place	Date	Hour	Summary of Events and Information	Remarks and references to Appendices
	November			
	17th.		In billets in LIESSIES.	
	18th.		In billets in LIESSIES. The Battalion paraded in the policies of the Chateau de la Motte, LEISSIES, at 14.00. The Commanding Officer referred to the work accomplished and the Battles fought on the soil of FRANCE. Before crossing the frontier, he desired the Battalion to pay the last mark of respect to the fallen Heroes of the Battalion who had laid down their lives in the great cause for which it had nobly fought. arms were presented, the buglers sounding the Last Post. Thereafter Pipe-Major McCombe played 'The Flowers of the Forest' and 'Lochaber no more'. After explaining the arrangements for the march into Germany as part of the Army of occupation, the Battalion was dismissed. Lieutenant P.H. BERTRAM joined the Battalion on this date.	
	19th		In billets in LIESSIES. The Battalion moved to billets in SIVRY.	
	20th		In billets in SIVRY. The Battalion moved to billets in FOURBECHIES.	
	21st		In billets in FOURBECHIES.	
	22nd		-do-	
	23rd		-do-	
	24th		-do- The Battalion moved to billets in CERFONTAINE.	
	25th		In billets in CERFONTAINE.	
	26th		-do-	

WAR DIARY or INTELLIGENCE SUMMARY.

Army Form C. 2118.

Place	Date	Hour	Summary of Events and Information	Remarks and references to Appendices
	27th		In billets in CERFONTAINE. Under Authority delegated by the Field - Marshal Commanding - in - Chief, the Corps Commander has awarded the following decorations :- **Bar to Military Medal.** No. 13181 Sergt G. SMITH, M.M. **The Military Medal.** No. 35097 Sergt R. ARCHIBALD. No. 16192 L/Cpl H. McKILLOP. No. 355510 L/Cpl F. SIMPSON. No. 35283 Pte J.R. ALLAN. No. 40505 Sgt J. ROBERTSON. No. 43118 Sergt J. ALLISON. No. 40078 Cpl T.C. JOHNSTON. No. 3398 Pte A. ANDERSON. No. 17059 L/Cpl H. McBRIDE. No. 14922 Pte M. ARMSTRONG. No. 27348 Pte J. ORMISTON. No. 33120 Pte W. CHAPPELL. No. 30235 L/Cpl A. YOUNG. No. 30330 Pte J. GIBSON. No. 15258 Pte A. COLLINS. No. 52802 Cpl O. MACE. No. 42000 L/Cpl R. WALKER. No. 14715 Pte J.J. McGOWAN. No. 42326 Pte J.I. CAIRNS. No. 15839 L/Cpl D. MURRAY. No. 3383 C.Q.M.S. J. FORBES.	
	28th		In billets in CERFONTAINE. The Battalion worked on the roads in the vicinity of the village.	
	29th		In billets in CERFONTAINE. The Battalion paraded at 09.30 in front of the school and the Commanding Officer presented medal ribbons to the N.C.O's and Men who had been awarded the Military Medal in connection with the operations of bridging the SAMBRE - OISE Canal on the 4th November.	

Army Form C. 2118.

WAR DIARY
or
INTELLIGENCE SUMMARY.

(Erase heading not required.)

Instructions regarding War Diaries and Intelligence Summaries are contained in F. S. Regs., Part II. and the Staff Manual respectively. Title pages will be prepared in manuscript.

Place	Date	Hour	Summary of Events and Information	Remarks and references to Appendices
	30th		In billets in CERFONTAINE. This being ST ANDREW'S Day, the members of the Battalion wore small national flags kindly presented by the St Andrew's Society (Glasgow). A Scottish Concert was given by members of the Battalion at 18.00 in the hall in the school here.	

R.Rhyle Lieut-Colonel,
Commanding, 16th Bn The Highland Light Infantry.

WD 37

36 P
11 sheets

Confidential

War Diary
of the
16th Battalion The Highland Light Infantry

Volume XXXVIII

From 1st to 31st December, 1918

Volume XXXVIII Page 1.

WAR DIARY
or
INTELLIGENCE SUMMARY.
(Erase heading not required.)

Army Form C. 2118.

Instructions regarding War Diaries and Intelligence Summaries are contained in F. S. Regs., Part II. and the Staff Manual respectively. Title pages will be prepared in manuscript.

Place	Date 1918 Dec.	Hour	Summary of Events and Information	Remarks and references to Appendices
CERFONTAINE	1st.		In billets in CERFONTAINE, BELGIUM.	Obas?
CERFONTAINE	2nd.		In billets in CERFONTAINE, BELGIUM.	Obas?
CERFONTAINE	3rd.		In billets in CERFONTAINE, BELGIUM.	Obas?
CERFONTAINE	4th.		In billets in CERFONTAINE, BELGIUM.	Obas?
CERFONTAINE	5th.		In billets in CERFONTAINE, BELGIUM. The Battalion moved from billets in CERFONTAINE to billets in FLORENNES	Obas?
FLORENNES	6		In billets in FLORENNES. The Battalion moved from billets in FLORENNES to billets in BIOUL	Obas?

Volume XXXVIII Page 2

Army Form C. 2118.

WAR DIARY
or
INTELLIGENCE SUMMARY.
(Erase heading not required.)

Instructions regarding War Diaries and Intelligence Summaries are contained in F. S. Regs., Part II. and the Staff Manual respectively. Title pages will be prepared in manuscript.

Place	Date	Hour	Summary of Events and Information	Remarks and references to Appendices
BIOUL	1918 Dec. 7th		In billets in BIOUL. The Battalion moved from billets in BIOUL to billets in NANINNES. The following is a copy of a letter received by the Divisional Commander from the IX Corps Commander:— "I am so sorry that your gallant Division "is leaving the IX Corps. I thought you were "safe to stay with us, but the powers that "be have decided otherwise. "I would like to express to you personally "and to your Division my very real appreciation "of all the good work and hard fighting you have "done while with the Corps. You came with a "splendid reputation, and you have kept — "indeed enhanced — it. "I wish you all the best of good fortune. (Signed) Walter Braithwaite	Olvd

Army Form C. 2118.

Volume XXXVIII Page 3

WAR DIARY
or
INTELLIGENCE SUMMARY.

(Erase heading not required.)

Instructions regarding War Diaries and Intelligence Summaries are contained in F. S. Regs., Part II. and the Staff Manual respectively. Title pages will be prepared in manuscript.

Place	Date 1918 Dec.	Hour	Summary of Events and Information	Remarks and references to Appendices
NANINNES	8th		In billets in NANINNES	
			The following Officers joined the Battalion:-	
			Lieut. J. McLellan, MC, from tour of duty in United Kingdom	
			2 Lieut. A.G. Cockburn from 1/5th H/L/I	Checked
NANINNES	9th		In billets in NANINNES	
			"A" Company moved to billets in MAIZERET to work on Horse Standings for Divisional Artillery. "C" Company moved to billets in SAR BERNARD to work on Horse Standings for Divisional Ammunition Column.	
			"B" Company working on Horse Standings for Divisional Artillery	Checked
NANINNES	10th		Headquarters and "B" Company in billets in NANINNES	
			"A" Company in billets in MAIZERET at work on Horse Standings	
			"C" Company on billets in SAR BERNARD at work on Horse Standings	Checked

Volume **XXXVIII** Page 4

Army Form C. 2118.

WAR DIARY
or
INTELLIGENCE SUMMARY.
(Erase heading not required.)

Instructions regarding War Diaries and Intelligence Summaries are contained in F.S. Regs., Part II. and the Staff Manual respectively. Title pages will be prepared in manuscript.

Place	Date 1918 M.C.	Hour	Summary of Events and Information	Remarks and references to Appendices
NANINNES	11th		Headquarters and "B" Company in NANINNES	
			"A" Company in MAIZERET "C" Company in SAR BERNARD	Obed
			Companies employed at work on Arty Standings for Divisional Artillery	
NANINNES	12th		Headquarters and "B" Company in NANINNES	
			"A" Company in MAIZERET "C" Company in SAR BERNARD	Obed
NANINNES	13th		Headquarters and "B" Company in NANINNES	
			"A" Company in MAIZERET "C" Company in SAR BERNARD	Obed
NANINNES	14th		Headquarters and "B" Company in NANINNES	
			"A" Company in MAIZERET "C" Company in SAR BERNARD	Obed
			Headquarters and "B" Company moved to Billets in MAILLEN	

Volume XXXVIII Page 5

Army Form C. 2118.

WAR DIARY
or
INTELLIGENCE SUMMARY.
(Erase heading not required.)

Instructions regarding War Diaries and Intelligence Summaries are contained in F. S. Regs., Part II. and the Staff Manual respectively. Title pages will be prepared in manuscript.

Place	Date 1918	Hour	Summary of Events and Information	Remarks and references to Appendices
MAILLEN	Dec. 15th		Headquarters and "B" Company in MAILLEN	
			"A" Company in MAIZERET "C" Company in SAK BERNARD	
			Under Authority delegated by His Majesty the King, the Fields Marshal Commanding-in-Chief	
			has awarded the following decoration	
			The Military Cross	
			Lieut. W. J. Watson	Olens?
MAILLEN	16th		Headquarters and "B" Company in MAILLEN	
			"A" Company in MAIZERET "C" Company in SAK BERNARD	
			The following letter was received from the Division:-	
			The Field Marshal Commanding-in-Chief, accompanied by the Chief of the General Staff and	
			the G.O.C. Fourth Army visited Divisional Headquarters on Sunday 15th December.	
			After referring to the many severe actions through which he has watched the successful progress of	
			the Division, especially since 8th August, 1918, the Field Marshal desired the Divisional Commander to convey	
			to all ranks his personal appreciation of their great services and of their gallantry, and his thanks for	
			the behaviour which has at all times distinguished the Division.	

Volume XXXVIII Page 6

Army Form C. 2118.

WAR DIARY
or
INTELLIGENCE SUMMARY.
(Erase heading not required.)

Instructions regarding War Diaries and Intelligence Summaries are contained in F. S. Regs., Part II. and the Staff Manual respectively. Title pages will be prepared in manuscript.

Place	Date	Hour	Summary of Events and Information	Remarks and references to Appendices
MAILLEN.	1918 Dec. 16th		He sent to all ranks his heartiest good wishes for a Happy Christmas and New Year.	(Nent?)
MAILLEN	17th		Headquarters and "B" Coy in Billets in MAILLEN "A" Company in billets in MAIZERET "C" Coy in billets in SAI. BERNARD "C" Company moved to billets in LES TOMBES to work on three standings for No 2. Section Divisional Ammunition Column.	(Nent?)
MAILLEN	18th		Headquarters and "B" Coy in Billets in MAILLEN A. Company in billets in MAIZERET "C" Company in billets in LES TOMBES	(Nent?)
MAILLEN	19th		Headquarters and "B" Coy in billets in MAILLEN A. Company in billets in MAIZERET "C" Company in billets in LES TOMBES	(Nent?)

Volume XXXVIII Page 7.

Army Form C. 2118.

WAR DIARY
or
INTELLIGENCE SUMMARY.
(Erase heading not required.)

Place	Date Hour	Summary of Events and Information	Remarks and references to Appendices
MAILLEN	1918 Dec. 20th	Headquarters and "B" Company in billets in MAILLEN	
		"A" Company in MAIZERET "C" Company in LES TOMBES	
		Under authority granted by His Majesty the King, the Field Marshal Commanding in Chief has awarded the following decorations:-	
		The Military Cross	
		2nd Lieut. J.L. Young. M.6.M.M.M.	
		Lieut. E.W.M. Heddle	
		The Distinguished Conduct Medal	
		No.44192 Sergt McCoskley	
		9032 Pte A Fraser	
		12298 LCpl T Galloway	
		14659 Pte J. Beattie	
		34789 Pte J. Kolio	Cleard

WAR DIARY
or
INTELLIGENCE SUMMARY.
(Erase heading not required.)

Army Form C. 2118.

Vinne XXXVIII Page 8

Instructions regarding War Diaries and Intelligence Summaries are contained in F. S. Regs., Part II. and the Staff Manual respectively. Title pages will be prepared in manuscript.

Place	Date	Hour	Summary of Events and Information	Remarks and references to Appendices
MAILLEN	21st		Headquarters and "B" Coy in MAILLEN	
			"A" Coy in billets in MAIZERET "C" Coy in LES TOMBES	
			"D" Company march to billets in COURRIERES	Obers
			"C" Company moved to billets in MAILLEN	
MAILLEN	22nd		In billets in MAILLEN	
			"A" Company in COURRIERES	Obers
MAILLEN	23rd		In billets in MAILLEN	
			A Company in COURRIERES	
			The following Officer joins the Battalion:-	
			Lieut. J. Miller from tour of duty in United Kingdom	Obers
MAILLEN	24th		In billets in MAILLEN	
			"A" Company in COURRIERES	Obers

Volume XXXVIII Page 9.

Army Form C. 2118.

WAR DIARY
or
INTELLIGENCE SUMMARY.
(Erase heading not required.)

Instructions regarding War Diaries and Intelligence Summaries are contained in F.S. Regs., Part II. and the Staff Manual respectively. Title pages will be prepared in manuscript.

Place	Date 1919 Dec.	Hour	Summary of Events and Information	Remarks and references to Appendices
MAILLEN	25th		In billets in MAILLEN	Nov. 1
			"A" Company in billets in COURRIERES	
MAILLEN	26th		In billets in MAILLEN	Nov. 1
			"A" Company in billets in COURRIERES	
MAILLEN	27th		In billets in MAILLEN	
			"A" Company in billets in COURRIERES	
			The following message from Lieut-General C.D.SHUTE, C.B., C.M.G. Commanding V Corps was received by the Divisional Commander:-	
			"Please congratulate all ranks of my old Division on all their splendid work, and wish them from me, a very Happy Christmas and a Happy and lucky New Year in 1919	
			(Sd) Cameron Shute Lieut-General	
			The following reply was sent:-	
			All ranks of 33rd Division thank you for your kind message and send Best Wishes for the New Year.	Nov. 1

WAR DIARY
or
INTELLIGENCE SUMMARY

Army Form C. 2118.

Volume XXXVIII Page 10

Place	Date 1918 Dec.	Hour	Summary of Events and Information	Remarks and references to Appendices
MAILLEN	28th		In billets in MAILLEN	Ol.u.P
			"A" Company in billets in COURRIERES	
MAILLEN	29th		In billets in MAILLEN	Ol.u.P
			"A" Company in billets in COURRIERES	
MAILLEN	30th		In billets in MAILLEN	Ol.u.P
			"A" Company in billets in COURRIERES	
MAILLEN	31st		In billets in MAILLEN	Ol.u.P
			"A" Company in billets in COURRIERES	

31st December 1918.

R. Doyle Lieut-Colonel.
Commanding 16th High. L.I.

LANCASHIRE DIVISION
(LATE 32ND DIVN)

16 H.L.I.
Jan - Feb '19

16TH BN HIGH'D LT INFY.
(PIONEERS)
JAN - FEB 1919

War Diary

of the

16th Battalion The Highland Light Infantry

Volume XXXIX

From 1st to 31st January 1919.

Volume XXXIX   Page 1

Army Form C. 2118.

WAR DIARY
or
INTELLIGENCE SUMMARY.

(Erase heading not required.)

Instructions regarding War Diaries and Intelligence Summaries are contained in F. S. Regs., Part II. and the Staff Manual respectively. Title pages will be prepared in manuscript.

Place	Date 1919 January	Hour	Summary of Events and Information	Remarks and references to Appendices
MAILLEN	1st		In billets in MAILLEN near NAMUR	nil
MAILLEN	2nd		In billets in MAILLEN near NAMUR. The Field Marshal Commanding in Chief under authority delegated by His Majesty the King has awarded the following decoration:- The Military Cross Captain T.E. Harris (New Years Honours despatch)	nil
MAILLEN	3rd		In billets in MAILLEN near NAMUR The Fox	nil
MAILLEN	4th		In billets in MAILLEN near NAMUR The Field Marshal Commanding in Chief under authority delegated by His Majesty the King has awarded the following decorations:- Distinguished Conduct Medal New Years Honours despatch No. 14132 To Sm. P. Halliwell	nil

Volume XXXIX Page 2

Army Form C. 2118.

WAR DIARY
or
INTELLIGENCE SUMMARY.
(Erase heading not required.)

Instructions regarding War Diaries and Intelligence Summaries are contained in F. S. Regs., Part II. and the Staff Manual respectively. Title pages will be prepared in manuscript.

Place	Date 1919 January	Hour	Summary of Events and Information	Remarks and references to Appendices
MAILLEN	5th		In billets in MAILLEN near NAMUR	nil
do	6th		In billets in MAILLEN	nil
do	7th		In billets in MAILLEN	nil
do	8th		In billets in MAILLEN. Lieut Colonel R.Kyle, D.S.O. proceeded to UK today on one months leave. Major W.B.Tait, D.S.O, M.C. assumed Command of the Battalion	nil
do	9th		In billets in MAILLEN	nil
do	10th		In billets in MAILLEN	nil
do	11th		In billets in MAILLEN	nil

Army Form C. 2118.

WAR DIARY
or
INTELLIGENCE SUMMARY.
(Erase heading not required.)

Volume XXXIX Page 3

Instructions regarding War Diaries and Intelligence Summaries are contained in F. S. Regs., Part II. and the Staff Manual respectively. Title pages will be prepared in manuscript.

Place	Date 1914 January	Hour	Summary of Events and Information	Remarks and references to Appendices
MAILLEN	12th		In billets in MAILLEN near NAMUR	
MAILLEN	13th		In billets in MAILLEN	
do	14th		In billets in MAILLEN	
do	15th		In billets in MAILLEN	
do	16th		In billets in MAILLEN	
do	17th		In billets in MAILLEN	
do	18th		In billets in MAILLEN	
do	19th		In billets in MAILLEN	

Volume XXXIX Page 4

WAR DIARY
or
INTELLIGENCE SUMMARY.

Army Form C. 2118.

Place	Date	Hour	Summary of Events and Information	Remarks and references to Appendices
MAILLEN	1919 20th		In billets in MAILLEN near NAMUR	
			The Field Marshal Commanding-in-Chief under authority delegated by His Majesty the King has awarded the following Accrations:-	
			The Meritorious Service Medal New Years Honours dispatch	
			No 14101 C.Q.M.S. J Aitken	
			No 14631 " D. Tarbitt	
			No 15038 Sgt H. McIntyre	
			No 350165 Pte W. Barndt	
Do	21st		In billets in MAILLEN near NAMUR	auy.
Do	22nd		In billets in MAILLEN near NAMUR	auy.
Do	23rd		In billets in MAILLEN near NAMUR	auy.

Volume XXXIX Page 5

Army Form C. 2118.

WAR DIARY
or
INTELLIGENCE SUMMARY.
(Erase heading not required.)

Place	Date 1919 January	Hour	Summary of Events and Information	Remarks and references to Appendices
MAILLEN	24th		Infillth in MAILLEN near NAMUR	
	25th		The Battalion was visited by HRH The Prince of Wales on this date	
Do	26th		Infillth in MAILLEN near NAMUR	
Do	27th		Infillth in MAILLEN	
Do	28th		Infillth in MAILLEN	
Do	29th		Infillth in MAILLEN	
Do	30th		Infillth in MAILLEN	
Do	31st		Infillth in MAILLEN	

Volume XXXIX page 6

WAR DIARY
or
INTELLIGENCE SUMMARY.

Army Form C. 2118.

(Erase heading not required.)

Place	Date	Hour	Summary of Events and Information	Remarks and references to Appendices
MAILLEN	1919 January 31st		Installed in MAILLEN near NAMUR. The Battalion moved from MAILLEN to MARIECHE	appx.

W. D. Scott
Major
Commanding 16th High. L.I.

31st January 1919

Ao⁰ 39

96/8 39

Confidential

Transport E pier 25/2/19.

War Diary
of the
16th Battalion The Highland Light Infantry
Volume XL

From 1st. to 28th. February 1919.

87 P
10 sheets

Volume XL Page 1

Army Form C. 2118.

WAR DIARY
or
INTELLIGENCE SUMMARY.
(Erase heading not required.)

Instructions regarding War Diaries and Intelligence Summaries are contained in F. S. Regs., Part II. and the Staff Manual respectively. Title pages will be prepared in manuscript.

Place	Date 1919 Feby.	Hour	Summary of Events and Information	Remarks and references to Appendices
MAMÊCHE	1st		In billets in MAMÊCHE near NAMUR, BELGIUM.	
			The Battalion entrained at MAMÊCHE, and proceeded by rail to BONN, GERMANY.	
			On arrival in BONN the Battalion marched to Billets in RHEINDORF	
RHEINDORF	2nd		In billets in RHEINDORF	
Do	3rd		Do	
Do	4th		Do	
Do	5th		Massed Pipe bands of the Division played Retreat in the KAISERPLATZ, BONN.	
Do	6th		Do	
Do	7th		Do	

Army Form C. 2118.

Volume XL Page 2

WAR DIARY
or
INTELLIGENCE SUMMARY.
(Erase heading not required.)

Instructions regarding War Diaries and Intelligence Summaries are contained in F. S. Regs., Part II. and the Staff Manual respectively. Title pages will be prepared in manuscript.

Place	Date 1919 Feby	Hour	Summary of Events and Information	Remarks and references to Appendices
RHEINDORF	8th		In billets in RHEINDORF	
Do	9th		Do	
Do	10th		Do	
Do	11th		Do Lieut Colonel R.Kyd. M.C. rejoined the Battalion from leave on this date	
DOTTENDORF	12th		The Battalion moved to billets in DOTTENDORF. In billets in DOTTENDORF near BONN, GERMANY. The Battalion Pipe Band played Retreat on the KAISERPLATZ, BONN	
Do	13th		Do Massed Pipe Bands of the Division played Retreat on the KAISERPLATZ, BONN	
Do	14th		Do	
Do	15th		Do Massed Pipe Bands of the Division played Retreat on the KAISERPLATZ, BONN	

Army Form C 2118

War Diary

Volume XL. Page 3.

Place	1919 Febry	Hour	Summary of Events and Information	Remarks & references to Appendices
DOTTENDORF			Infillets in DOTTENDORF, near BONN, GERMANY	
Do	16th			
Do	17th		Do	
Do	18th		Do	
Do	19th		Do Massed Pipe Bands played in the KAISERPLATZ, BONN.	
Do	20th		Do The Pipe Band of the Battalion played Retreat in the KAISERPLATZ, BONN.	
Do	21st		Do	
Do	22nd		Do	
			His Majesty the King presented the Battalion with a King's Colour, and this was handed over by Lieut General Sir R.B. Stephens. K.G.B, G.M.G., Commanding the 10th Corps. The Ceremony took place in the Hofgarten, BONN at 1000 hours. The Battalion was drawn up on three sides of a square, with the university of BONN in the background. The Colour Party under command of Lieut James Miller was :— No.15190 Sergt Mc Clark. No.14516 Sergt T.Bligh No.16104 A/Cpl H. Andrews No.14999 A/L/Cpl H.Crawford The cased colour was brought forward by No.14597 RSM G.J. Taylor. M.C. and uncased by the 2nd in command Major W.T. Scott. S.T.O. M.C. The Colour was consecrated, the officiating clergyman being the Rev Archibald McHardy, C.F. After Major General Lambert, C.B, C.M.G. Commanding 32nd Division had given an address on the history of the Battalion, the colour was received from General Stephens by Lieut James Miller. Notwithstanding the inclement weather a very large gathering of people witnessed the ceremony. During the Ceremony the Corps Commander made the following remarks:—	

Volume XL Page 4

Army Form C. 2118.

WAR DIARY
or
INTELLIGENCE SUMMARY.

(Erase heading not required.)

Instructions regarding War Diaries and Intelligence Summaries are contained in F. S. Regs., Part II. and the Staff Manual respectively. Title pages will be prepared in manuscript.

Place	Date 1919	Hour	Summary of Events and Information	Remarks and references to Appendices
DOTTENDORF	22nd		"Colonel Hope, Officers, N.C.O's and men of the 16th Highland Light Infantry. I am here this morning to hand over to you the colours which has been presented to you by His Majesty the King in recognition of the magnificent service which you have rendered during the War."	
			"Your Divisional Commander has just read out the record of what you have done. It is a record of which any Regiment, at any period in the history of the our, the Army would be proud."	
			"You are a young Battalion of a very glorious old Regiment. On the colours of your Regular Battalions are inscribed many Battle honours gained in India, in the Peninsula, at Waterloo, in the Crimea and elsewhere, but I think that the Campaign which you have recently helped to bring to a successful conclusion, has shown harder fighting and greater losses than any that preceded it. It has forced again, if proof was required, that the British Infantry are the best fighting troops in the World. In this Campaign your Battalion has played no small part. Its Infantry on the SOMME, at BEAUMONT HAMEL, at PASSCHENDAELE and many other places you were in the hardest fighting in the War.	

Volume II. Page 5.

WAR DIARY
or
INTELLIGENCE SUMMARY.

Army Form C. 2118.

Place	Date	Hour	Summary of Events and Information	Remarks and references to Appendices
DÜTTENDORF	22nd		"To honour your work has been no less strenuous and your work in the bridging of the SOMME and of the canals at BELLENGLISE and OISE was masterly.	
			The Colour which I have handed to you today is a proof that His Majesty the King recognises that your deeds in this War are as great as those of your predecessors in the old Battalions."	
			"The Colour is more than that, it is a symbol of the Honour of your Regiment. In the old days when it was carried into action, it was a rallying point for the Battalion. To-day it the most gallant deeds have been done, and it has led the most glorious attacks. Although owing to modern conditions, it is no longer carried into the fight it still represents the Honour of the Regiment and is for you an emblem of your loyalty to King and Country."	
			"The victory that you have helped to win is an immense one. The proof of it is that I am handing you this colour in one of Germany's best known towns, and within sight of one of her greatest universities. But let us remember that this victory has been won by the very qualities which your colour represents – the qualities of self sacrifice and devotion to duty."	

Volume II. Page 6

WAR DIARY
or
INTELLIGENCE SUMMARY

Army Form C. 2118.

Place	Date	Hour	Summary of Events and Information	Remarks and references to Appendices
DOTTENDORF	1919 Feby	22nd	"Also let us remember that this victory was not won by us who stand here today, but in greater part by our many comrades who have given their lives for the great cause."	
			In memory of them and in thankfulness for the victory, let me ask you who are here today to pledge yourselves whether as Soldiers in the Army or as citizens of our Great Empire, never to forget the honour of your regiment and your loyalty to King and Country.	
			Reply from Lieut Colonel R. Hoyle. D.S.O. Comdg 16th H.L.I. :-	
			General Stephens.-	
			On behalf of the Battalion I wish to thank you for the honour you have done us in presenting this Colour, the gift of His Most Gracious Majesty the King.	
			I can assure you it will be jealously guarded by us so long as the Battalion exists.	
			When we have fulfilled our destiny and become demobilized, the colour will be handed to the great city which brought us into being, and I trust it will accord a resting place in some Ancient Cathedral because for you have said, it is worthy of a place among the colours of past generations of Scottish Soldiers and thus adorn the walls of that sacred building. Aitha	
			Conclusion of the ceremony the Battalion marched back to billets through BONN with fixed bayonets	

Volume XI. Page 7.

Army Form C. 2118.

WAR DIARY
or
INTELLIGENCE SUMMARY.
(Erase heading not required.)

Place	Date 1919 February	Hour	Summary of Events and Information	Remarks and references to Appendices
DOTTENDORF	23rd		In Billets in DOTTENDORF, near BONN, GERMANY. The Battalion attended Church in the Protestant Church, KAISERPLATZ, BONN. General W. Lambert, C.B., CMG., and Staff attended. He was the first occasion the Battalion has worshipped in a church since coming overseas in November, 1915.	
DOTTENDORF	24th		Do. The following Special Order of the day was issued from 32nd Division:— "In bidding farewell to the 16th Battalion The Highland Light Infantry on 25th February, I desire to thank all ranks for the loyalty, devotion and energy which they have at all times displayed, especially during the last nine months during which I have had the honour to command the 32nd Division. It was these qualities which maintained the spirit of the Division through times of greatest difficulty and trial, and which led us to victory throughout the great advance from 8th August till the Armistice in November." The Battalion on the British Army can show ample examples of sentiment known than was displayed at BEAUMONT HAMEL on 18th November, 1916, where 60 N.C.O.s and men of the 16th H.L.I. were cut off after reaching their objective, but held out for six days, during 2 of which they were without food. The outstanding work done by the Battalion, and especially the unsuccessful crossing, in conjunction with the Royal Engineers, of the SOMME, the ST QUENTIN CANAL, and	

Volume XI   Page 8

Army Form C. 2118.

WAR DIARY
or
INTELLIGENCE SUMMARY.
(Erase heading not required.)

Place	Date 1919 February	Hour	Summary of Events and Information	Remarks and references to Appendices
DOTTENDORF	24th		the SAMBRE-OISE CANAL often under heavy fire, and despite many casualties, showed the determination of the Battalion to take its full share in all the victories of the Division. Glasgow may well be proud of the troops it has raised, and of the men it has so fully given to the Honour of our King and Country. The presentation of Colours in Brussels, to the two Battalions on the eve of their departure to join the Lowland Division, forms a fitting termination to the services which they have rendered during the War, to their King and Country, and to the glory of the 52nd Division. For myself no honour can be higher than that of having served with them in the Division, and having helped to lead them to final victory. In the name of the 32nd Division, Lieut-Colonel Kyle, D.S.O., Commanding 16th Battalion H.L.I., to convey to all ranks my thanks for their services and my best wishes for their happy future in the Army of the Rhine.	[signature]
DOTTENDORF	25th		In billets in DOTTENDORF, near BONN, GERMANY. The Battalion entrained at BONN and moved by rail to SOLINGEN and came under orders of G.O.C. 9th Division, under whose command the Lowland Lothian Brigade was being formed.	[signature]

A.I.C. 2118.

Volume XL Page 9

War Diary

Place	1919 February Hour	Summary of Events and Information
SOLINGEN	26th	In billets in SOLINGEN, GERMANY.
Do	27th	Do " " " "
Do	28th	Do " " " "

28th February 1919.

R. H. Kyle
Lieut-Colonel
Commanding 16th H.L.I.

www.ingramcontent.com/pod-product-compliance
Lightning Source LLC
Chambersburg PA
CBHW081433160426
43193CB00013B/2271